Marx Adolf Bernhard

Introduction to the Interpretation of the Bethoven Piano Works

.

Marx Adolf Bernhard

Introduction to the Interpretation of the Bethoven Piano Works

ISBN/EAN: 9783744796026

Printed in Europe, USA, Canada, Australia, Japan

Cover: Foto ©Thomas Meinert / pixelio.de

More available books at **www.hansebooks.com**

INTRODUCTION

TO THE INTERPRETATION
OF THE

BEETHOVEN PIANO WORKS

BY

ADOLF BERNHARD MARX.

TRANSLATED BY

FANNIE LOUISE GWINNER,

Instructor in Pianoforte in Iowa College Conservatory,
Grinnell, Iowa.

PUBLISHED BY

CLAYTON F. SUMMY CO.
220 Wabash Ave., Chicago.

TRANSLATOR'S PREFACE.

THE value of Marx's Introduction to the Interpretation of Beethoven's Piano Works has been widely recognized, and this recognition has been accompanied by universal regret at its inaccessibility, except to the limited few who are sufficiently conversant with German for satisfactory perusal of the contents.

There has been a very apparent deficiency and superficiality in the study of Beethoven's pianoforte compositions, possibly because of their technical difficulties, but more because of a lack of appreciation of their real thought and content; perhaps, too, a fear of the technical may have prevented a clear insight into their soul life. Again, they have been mutilated by an attempt on the part of virtuosos to transform them into bravura pieces, which most certainly they are not, and their meaning, of necessity, became obliterated. We have numerous players and teachers who have devoted themselves to other composers, but very few have given their main thought to Beethoven; and yet it cannot be disputed that his compositions comprise the greatest variety, from deepest pathos to most sparkling humor, never failing, however, to manifest the one soul which pervades them all. Indeed, their study not only leads into higher realms of imagination, but it prepares for all that can be found in pianoforte literature.

That Marx was the most able commentator of Beethoven is beyond a doubt; and certainly his clear presentation of the larger works which have been "as sounding brass" to so many able musicians, as well as his classification of the smaller ones, must be invaluable to students of Beethoven. Added to this, is his exposition of playing in general, of the various legato and staccato qualities which have been a sealed book to the majority of music students. The oft-quoted phrase, "We play too much and think too little," is here so elucidated as to guide even a careless thinker.

To those from whom this book has been withheld, and who desire to avail themselves of Marx's guidance, this translation is dedicated. I have endeavored to retain as far as possible the original phraseology of the author, which is too strong to bear much interpolation; but I have striven assiduously to avoid transposed German into English, and have therefore been compelled to use free translation now and then, especially in order not to interfere with the clearness of the thought.

I wish to express my most hearty thanks to Mr. Calvin B. Cady, both for his earnest efforts in leading me to a sufficient comprehension of Beethoven's work to desire to undertake this translation, and also for his invaluable assistance in editing the same during its publication in the *Music Review*, previous to its appearance in book form.   FANNIE LOUISE GWINNER.

Ann Arbor, Michigan, August, 1894.

PREFACE TO THE FIRST EDITION.

THE first edition of my Biography of Beethoven—"Beethoven, Life and Work"—was accompanied by an Appendix: "A few remarks concerning the study and interpretation of the Beethoven piano works." This Appendix was inspired by love for Beethoven, and the conviction that without a deep comprehension of his creations, a thorough comprehension of the tonal art is out of the question; but in the very writing of the same, it became evident that nothing satisfactory could be done within so limited a compass.

Now with the second edition of the Biography, opportunity is furnished for solving the problem more satisfactorily. The Biography, thanks to invaluable information which has come to me from many sources, has appeared in a larger form; and the Introduction to Interpretation could no longer remain in the background, nor could it continue to be casually thrown in as Appendix.

It appears as an individual work, and will be useful by itself. Furthermore, the inner relationship between the Introduction and the Biography will be recognized by those who have become convinced that works of art can only be fully comprehended through the thought and life of the composer. The Biography furnishes the necessary foundation for a comprehension of Beethoven and of his individual works, and also the essential proofs for the Introduction—in so far as these demonstrate the thought of the master.

The greatest benefit, of course, is derived from the student's own perseverance and poetic instinct, and this cannot be given either by the Introduction or by the Biography. The word of an instructor is like the voice of the herald; it is able to awaken, to excite, to guide, only when it resounds to open ears, and into ambitious, persevering minds.

Berlin, March 18, 1863.   ADOLF BERNHARD MARX.

The Preface to the second edition, from which this work is translated, is written by Gustav Behncke, who edited the same in 1875. He states that a revision was necessary only because of his revision of the Biography from which a part of this work was taken. Notes had been supplied here and there, and in order to make the two works coincide, a few changes had to be made here. The changes were, however, so unimportant as to their intrinsic value, that this second edition could hardly be considered a revised edition. He closes with the following: " This book is most warmly commended to every intelligent piano player who, in reproducing a piano composition, is not satisfied with simply conquering technical difficulties, and who, on the other hand is not willing to be dependent upon the dictates of his own subjectivity and transitory mood, but who is desirous of developing his performance from a deep, objective comprehension of the work. Guidance is here given by the most able connoisseur of Beethoven's spirit."   THE TRANSLATOR.

CONTENTS.

Introductory Remarks.

Friends—Strangers—Teachers.

Presupposition of knowledge and preparation -Guide to interpretation
—Its general advisability—Demand for a guide to interpretation of
Beethoven—Peculiar content of his works—Their individuality—The
peculiarities of one as compared with another.

Instruction through precept and example—Virtuosi and " Klaviermas-
ters "—How Beethoven is cast aside and how he is dealt with—Instruction through purely practical representation--Purely theoretic instruction.

1. Technique—Is virtuosity essential?—Beethoven's opinion of virtuosity
—Gradations of his works from a technical standpoint.
2. Spiritual maturity—Who is ready to study Beethoven?—Gradation
of his works according to development of spiritual maturity.

Elementary and art-aspiring technique—Especial difficulties found in
Beethoven—The Viennese instruments in Beethoven's time as compared
with those of the present—Conclusions drawn therefrom--The una
corda.

Progress of Technique since Beethoven—Departures from the general
rules of fingering—One-voiced figures divided between the two hands—
Two or more voices in one hand.

Tendency of the newer technique toward equalizing fingers—Necessity
of liberating hand from hand and finger from finger—Stroke—Position
of the hand.

How Beethoven's melody should be played--Difference between
Beethoven's melodies; complete as to close, and emphatic—How to
perceive it. How to represent it—Rhythmic accents.

Comprising: Accompaniment which contains no characteristic contents
within itself—Accompaniment with substantial but subordinate voices.
Polyphony.

Tempo--Older significance of the same—The metronome— Exaggeration of tempo--Mozart—Beethoven—How to find the correct tempo.
Rhythm--Rhythmic firmness. Rhythmic freedom. Meaning and demands of both—Beethoven's manner of playing in this respect—Preser-
vation of rhythmic feeling amid rhythmic freedom, through absence of
exaggeration; through return to tempo; through rhythmic intonation
and rhetorical pause.

Form of Study.. 80

GUIDE TO THE INDIVIDUAL WORKS.

THE READERS OF THE BOOK.

ONE who writes a book thinks occasionally of those whom he might desire as readers. I seek as readers for my little book those young people whose susceptible hearts have already been strongly moved at times by the harmonies of Beethoven; those that have been uplifted by these tones which have been heard like voices of prophecy from early youth — tones so new and strange and at the same time so primal and so intimate with our soul life. I would desire for my circle those pure-hearted youths, in whom, at the hearing of Beethoven's themes, an intimation has been awakened of the primal tones, primal melodies which constitute for our art the eternal, inexhaustible source; the divine reflections which all tone-poets believingly adhere to and seek after, which they strive to grasp, to their own delight and that of their hearers, but which have never been revealed to anyone more often or more powerfully than to the master.

I would desire those youths who still have open ears and hearts for the wonder tales of poets in word or tone; who, trusting and yielding with childlike simplicity, are gladly deceived and enticed because they divine in the deceptions of the poets eternal truths which are worth more than cold and destructive sophistry. Woe to those who are inaccessible to such happy deceptions! Therefore I would wish as readers those youths who still retain the belief that, in the midst of the drifting dust of everyday life with its duties and poverties, its sophistic and never-satisfying ends, its praiseworthy but dead industries, there blooms another life full of imperishable fragrance, of high thoughts and mighty deeds, whether they manifest themselves in the eye of love, in tones or words or pictures, or in the confident working for justice and freedom of men and peoples. For all this the master's heart has beaten, and has found assuring themes. Therefore are these youths allied and pledged to him who, even to his last bed of pain, had retained faith and youth.

But I would also desire those who have not yet recognized, but have heard of this wonderful man, who in the midst of a bubbling love of life and happiness of activity, was struck a blow by destiny which would have destroyed anyone else in his profession. History represents him as shattered, reeling under the stupefying stroke, cut off from the comforting play of his art, separated by invisible and unbreakable bonds from communion with man whom he loved, whose fraternity he longed for. He is burdened with the curse of undeserved and unavoidable mistrust and misdeed, yet in the midst of all distress he never loses his love for humanity, nor his consciousness of a high calling, and never ceases to work faithfully for it. Indeed, history whispers to us the secret that his tortures were the source and the inspiration of all his deepest revelations. Who, then, when this report has reached him, can deny himself entrance into this mystic world?

It has been written in past ages, that there will be more rejoicing over one who has been lost and is found, than over a hundred who have never been endangered. So I desire also those who for one reason or another have strayed from the path of pure art; those who, either through errors of their own or through erroneous guidance of others, have lost sight of that luminous summit, or possibly have never seen it. I desire those who, doubtful and not comprehending the mysteries and enigmatic words of the master, falter, hesitate, and finally content themselves with empty play in the low bushes by the wayside, thus wasting time and taste upon trivials, which art, directed to eternal truths, knows nothing of, and has no use for. They do not yet belong to the master. What a privilege to lift them with powerful hand out of the brambles, and to guide them by a happy word onward, leading them upon the path which they originally longed for, and where alone their desire for life in art can be gratified! Let them but gather courage to become acquainted with themselves and with their longings. For indeed, in every soul not radically turned away from art, there lives a representation of that enrichment and elevation of existence which only art accomplishes. This representation lives in every soul which has not entirely grown cold, even though it may be manifested only in indistinct sketches and paling colors. If temporary forgetfulness, relaxation, or deception have caused this turning away, then a word spoken in time will awaken the loiterer and remind the erring one. I have found this often enough in my teaching, as will every earnest teacher—and though none of us had ever tested it, we would nevertheless not doubt the power of Truth and of true being.

In conclusion, my most welcome, honored guests will be from

the ranks of teachers; those honored men who are not too proud or too set in their ways to listen and be taught; those who have a sufficiently high conception of their art to realize that the entire art, and the full perception thereof, is not locked up in one, as though placed in a holy shrine; but that we all, artists and teachers, the most proficient as well as the most humble, can be nothing more than co-workers in the one common cause. They know that through art we are brought into brotherhood—that none can do without the other, nor would wish to; and that the most remarkable teachers remain forever pupils, who dare not evade instruction and close their ears to the word of instructors, lest they fall from their calling and reduce themselves to poverty. Indeed, who ever finishes learning? Those who recognize this, and really act upon it, they are the true, honored men among teachers.

The appreciation of this is comparatively simple, the realization, however, is more difficult for many of us. Consider how we teachers have come together, and how we are placed: many from the lowest steps of fortune's ladder—bound to deprivation and poverty, from which merit does not always relieve them—oftenest only merit and good fortune bound in a mystical relationship. Others, again, are burdened with professional duties of all kinds. How can either of these obtain time, means, and concentration for study which requires not only these, but also strength and courage! Many a one has come stealthily into our circle, to whom before an entirely different career seemed allotted—the splendor of a path of virtuosity, until, through the intoxicating applause of concerts, he had become tired of such outer flitting life and was obliged to consider the wavering income. Others, again, creep reluctantly into our circle, away from the most delightful of all pleasures—the impetus to creative work, which strews heavenly manna; seldom, however, earthly bread—as was the experience of Mozart and Beethoven, and a hundred others in our fair Germany. Such impetus and desire throbs on in the heart even though the hope of youth has been deceptive. And is then the absence of success really a failure? Lessing has said, "A few are celebrated—others deserve to be." When a composer is not sufficiently recognized, it does not always follow that he was at variance with the art; more often it shows that he was not willing to buy sympathy by policy. Did not Æschylus, when the times became worse, banish himself from his fatherland?

Therefore, amid the whirl of life, to find courage and modesty and power to press on—that is truly worthy of honor.

THE CONTENTS OF THE BOOK.

Unto such readers and their friends, this little book offers itself as an adviser and guide in the mysteries of Beethoven. The essential thing is to conceive of his creations in his spirit, and to express them according to his thought, by means of the piano. A general essential knowledge as well as the necessary virtuosity is taken for granted. Only single hints can and should find access here. How many of these are necessary or beneficial to each individual person cannot be anticipated, as all depends upon the degree and character of the general preparation for pianoforte playing.

Thus the real purpose of the book is not to present a work directed to the study of interpretation in a general sense, but to that of Beethoven's works in particular. In how far it complies with the general rules of expression, and in what degree it goes above them requires no explanation—every intelligent reader will observe that of his own accord. Likewise we require no proof as to the need of such a work, for no one who has even a conception of art would be satisfied with simply playing the notes, he would desire to reproduce the thought of the composition. Notes, like the dead letters of words, manifest only inadequately the spirit of the composer. Of what avail are the few intensity marks from *pp* to *ff*, compared with the inexpressible shades of tone which are not only possible, but which really manifest themselves in rich numbers in every inspired performance!

How uncertain, too, are the verbal directions of time; how binding, enslaving, and inappropriate to circumstances and conditions are the metronomic indications! How far do they and the metric relationships fall short of the varied play of emotion of the enlightened interpreter, in whom free, full soul-life is reflected! We can easily see how little dependence the composer can place upon all conceivable signs and words, in order to lay open the live contents of his works, even if he were to paint his paper nearly black with them. After all that he may possibly have written down, he must depend upon the completing sympathy of the interpreter, and if this sympathy is wanting, he may justly sigh, "He has played all correctly from the notes, but he has not felt, not understood what I have wished to say."

We observe, then, that *all depends upon the perception of that which could not have been written down.* The foundation for all this—susceptibility for artistic representation—must be inborn, and from childhood instinctively developed. Where this requisite is wanting, neither script nor instruction can serve to make vital that which is lifeless. Natural talent alone, however, does not suffice; it must be developed and elevated, in order to reach above the bounds of self, and beyond to the work of art which must be perceived and represented. We wish also to have assurance that the natural feeling will lead to the desired end; that not the simply subjective or casual sensation of the interpreter, but the real thought of the work of art may be manifested. The purely subjective conception may suffice only when the work of art is within the limits of thought and expression common to all, in which each one understands and can make known what lives in all, and therefore in him. As soon, however, as the work of art rises above this generality, when it is no more common to all, but demands the expression of a more particular character, the subjective feeling no longer suffices, but the particular contents of the work and the means for its outward manifestation must be truly recognized. Hereby is designated the twofold mission of every study of interpretation.

At the same time it becomes clear for what reason Beethoven's works particularly require a guide to their interpretation. They require the same because their contents preëminently, and much more than the works of other masters, are of a nature peculiar to themselves; a nature which is not reached by a general subjective feeling as would suffice for the pianoforte works of other men, such as Haydn, Mozart, Dussek, Hummel, Chopin, Mendelssohn, and nearly all the others—with the exception only of a few works of John Sebastian Bach.

The peculiar content of Beethoven's style manifests itself in the fact that through his works, instrumental, and more particularly pianoforte music, attained to idealism and became the expression of determined ideal thought. Before this time they had been (with a few exceptions of Bach) only a graceful play of tone figures, or else a re-echoing of flitting and indefinite frames of mind.

Those who are drawn toward this sympathy and this toneplay are prepared for these works, which are consecrated to both.

If, however, very characteristic thoughts appear in the work, they cannot grasp them and present them comprehensively unless they comprehend their contents clearly and definitely.*

But even such of Beethoven's works in which no ideal content can be traced, distinguish themselves from the large majority of all others, (again with the exception of Bach) through the earnestness and endurance with which the master has developed them. Take, for example, the Sonatas Op. 22 and 53, and we find principally formal development. But how vastly is the form laid out! In what richly varied and thoughtful ways the musical ideas are used, reharmonized, and interwoven! Let us examine the first part of the D-major Sonata Op. 10. Observe how the little motive, *d, c-sharp, b, a,* works itself continually about, forming the first principal theme, reappearing again in the subordinate theme, or rather forming its principal substance. Now it excites all the voices; again it grows out of its puniness into a mighty bass theme, and finally twines itself throughout the whole rich movement. It would prove impossible to attain the comprehension of such a work (and the majority are like it) by depending only on one's talent, without thorough training and careful preparation.

The individually different character of Beethoven's instrumental, and more particularly pianoforte works, explains the reason why the works of other masters do not serve as a preparation toward the study of these, in the same degree with which they tend toward developing each other. Haydn and Clementi may lead into Mozart, however short Clementi may fall, and however distinctly different the peculiarities of these two German masters may be. Let us look further and we find Dussek and Louis-Ferdinand followed by A. E. Mueller, Wœlfl, Hummel, and many others of the Mozart type. Chopin, Weber, and Moscheles then appear as forerunners of Mendelssohn, Liszt, and Thalberg (and their number might be extended). All these lead up to one another, although each one asserts more or less individuality. One who comprehends Dussek will not be a stranger to Louis-Ferdinand; one who has made Thalberg his own has essentially mastered Henselt, and stands in closer relation to the incomparably spirituelle Liszt as well as the genial Robert Schu-

---

* In order to avoid endless repetitions I must be permitted to refer here and there in this work to my biography of Beethoven, "Beethoven's Life and Work." There my efforts were directed towards recognizing the artist from his works, and understanding them from his life and character; while here I wish to depict the practical presentation at the instrument. In other words, I shall consider here more minutely what I sought to do only in a general way in the other work.

mann — *the only one who has most often striven after Beethoven in earnestness and in truth.* We may know them all, and yet find ourselves in a new world with Beethoven.

In conclusion, it is seen that with him, one work does not ✓ even sufficiently prepare another. Whoever has conquered one work by Thalberg has gained the mastery of the arpeggios of all his compositions; and one who has learned to live in a few of Mozart's sonatas is equal to all others. Not so with Beethoven. The Symphonies 1, 2, 4, 8, guarantee by no means a comprehension of the Symphonies 3, 5, 6, 7, 9; the quartets, Op. 59, rise about as far above the Op. 18, as they fall short of the quartet Op. 132. The Sonatas Op. 22, 54, 53 stand as far off from those of Op. 27, 28, 81a, as the latter from those of Op. 106, 90, 101, 109 to 111. Each one from this incompletely combined list makes peculiar demands; hence each work must be individually conceived.

Beethoven gives in the list of his works a many-sided problem, but the gain is accordingly high and rich. We are lifted up into the ideal kingdom of art, and we gain through each work (with few exceptions) a new and peculiar perception. In proportion to the multiplicity of problems which Beethoven has solved, stands the number of works which a guide to interpretation must reach. At a hurried glance it would seem as though the works might be divided into classes according to their tendency toward (a) mere tone-form; (b) general feeling, or (c) clearly defined ideal content; and that the two former for more rapid classification might be disposed of together. Thus we might ascribe more of the tone-form character to the XXXII Variations in C minor, No. 36, the Concertos, with exception of the fourth, the Sonatas Op. 54, 22, 53; while to the Sonatas F minor Op. 2, F major Op. 10, E major Op. 14, F-sharp major Op. 78, the Fantasie Op. 77 indeterminate feeling might be attributed. As soon however as we go into them more deeply, we find that these and similar class divisions are not feasible. Hardly any work will follow strictly one certain direction; it will allow tone-play and emotion to intermingle, and gradually assume more determined character. Therefore we have no alternative but to go into the separate works so far as is necessary and practicable. We may exclude such works which, reviewed from a Beethoven standpoint, are of lesser worth, and therefore do not require individual guidance; such are:

I. All Variations, with exception of those of Op. 120; the

exemplary Variation-study No. 36 (XXXII Var. C Minor), also requires no directions.

II. All Concertos, Duos, and Trios, which certainly no one will undertake who has not worked up to them in a general way, through the study of pure pianoforte compositions.

III. The Bagatelles and other little pieces, the Fantasie Op. 77, the Sonatas Op. 6, Op. 49, the Sonatina Op. 79—works which on account of their slight value can hardly be called genuine, and which certainly require no special guidance.

Only occasional reference to single ones of these will find room here.

The principal subjects for this book will therefore be the Sonatas, with the exception of the above named. However, even these cannot all be considered, nor can they be examined sentence for sentence. Apart from the length of time and space required for such an undertaking, it would be neither necessary nor profitable. After a thing has been shown in one or more places, the student's own judgment must guide him in applying it in similar cases. In other words, his power of discrimination must be awakened and strengthened, and not allowed to become inactive by too much assistance.

METHODS OF INSTRUCTION.

THREE methods present themselves for instruction in expression: the representation at the instrument, the instructive word either oral or written, and the formal practical instruction which may combine verbal instruction and instrumental representation. The latter, based upon instruction and example, seems to be the most satisfactory and most true. Ah, if we only had competent teachers everywhere in sufficient numbers — instructors who are amply prepared for our purpose! They are rare, and always will be rare. The demands upon a music teacher are manifold, requiring not only a thorough insight into the technical development of the pupil, but an intelligent analysis of so many composers; hence it would be impossible to exact from each teacher that lifelong devotion to the study of Beethoven which this phenomenal man requires in order to be understood.

The many-sidedness of this demand, and the fatigue of daily teaching, is to the greater number of teachers the impenetrable barrier to becoming familiar with Beethoven's sphere, *i. e.*, the realm of thought. Many are incapable, others unwilling to follow him. Therefore from the beginning to the present day Beethoven has had opposition, especially in his pianoforte compositions, from those musicians whose standpoint lies outside of that realm. They are those who have given themselves principally, if not exclusively, to technique instead of to the ideal in art; the virtuosos* and the "clavier masters," as Beethoven himself names them in order to specify their technical aim. They are characterized by their undivided attention to Etudes, concert and salon pieces. For a while, long enough too, Beethoven's works were discarded by this circle as being not "piano-like," since, indeed, they do not find a place in the customary clipp-clapp mill of Etudes, and like mechanisms. Their spirit more often rises far above the wooden keys into representations of the orchestra, and even higher. One may be ever so thoroughly "practiced" in "tone-play," feel himself ever so firm in the saddle, and yet stumble in Beethoven, and that, too, in technically simple passages (as, for example, in the Sonata Op. 90); or light upon some unforeseen difficulty which, according to the

---

* "Thus each one grinds off what he himself has made," says Beethoven.

language of the technicians, is termed "thankless," that is, does not produce some startling or wonderful effect, nor often appear in the form of their daily food,—yclept Etudes—so that they do not offer a sufficient reward for the effort spent in mastering them.

But excuses of the above-named character will no longer be accepted, for Beethoven's spirit has become too powerful, not only among true musicians, but among people in general.

The study of Beethoven is generally promised for the future, but not until the student has become ready for this study. This is perfectly just, and will be discussed later on. This putting off can only be regarded as a sly escape in those teachers who neither determine what degree of preparation is required, nor earnestly labor toward its accomplishment. It is self-evident that such instructors cannot hope to lead to a ripeness for Beethoven, if they now and then rouse themselves out of heaps of other strange things and casually give themselves to the study of a few aimlessly chosen works. Among such, the Sonatas Op. 49 and 79, which cannot even be recognized as purely Beethovenish, figure above all others, also now and then one or another set of variations; not, however, the so-called "Bagatelles" (Op. 33), some of which give such excellent examples of his artistic depth and of his spiritual strength. Later on, the "Sonata Pathétique" is played. One who has not played anything else of Beethoven has certainly played the "Pathétique." The most skilled pupils are then given the C-sharp minor and F minor Sonatas, Op. 27 and 57, besides the C major Sonata, Op. 53, in addition to all the other Etudes and concert pieces. If the purpose might be judged of by the conception, these Sonatas serve them as excellent bravura and practice pieces. With the two first-named Sonatas, the custom began of carrying the Beethoven Sonatas into concerts.

As compared with actual instruction, purely theoretic instruction and practical representation stand in an undeniably similar relation. One gives advice and instruction without representing the thing itself; the other the exact opposite.

We all know the exciting and reviving power of the representation at the instrument. The work becomes a benefaction to the pupil, as soon as it comes to his hearing in its true sense. However, we must consider that in every performance of a work of art, through another but its creator, two things work together, namely, the thought which the creating artist manifests in it, and the subjectiveness of the performer. The latter is not even determinable, but is affected by momentary mood. Mood and subjectiveness cannot be excluded, no matter how conscientiously one strives to subordinate one's self to the idea of the work under consideration. Knowing that we may never expect to obtain a pure picture of the work from the performance of it, we must add to this argument, the speed of every musical execution. Think of how many feelings, thoughts, and thought-pictures crowd together in one or two quarters of an hour in which a Sonata Op. 101 or 106 hastens by, and our gain becomes still more doubtful. At the best, the attentive hearer is drawn to the thought of the performer, and follows him rather than his own thought and inclination. Or else these will sooner or later lead him to the point whereat theoretic education aims.

Purely theoretic instruction is devoid of all the charms and advantages of representation; while on the other hand, it has the inestimable advantage over the other, in that it awakens the pupil's spirit, reason, and phantasy—calling them into action and strengthening them. This is the essential thing in every branch of instruction, and remains the essential thing whatever may have been the method of instruction. Indeed, this method alone is powerful enough to demand of the pupil the completion of that which it has had to leave unfinished. If I should hear the Sonata Op. 106 ever so thoroughly, and should impress it on my mind ever so firmly, I still would not know a word of the Sonata Op. 101. If, on the other hand, I have strengthened reason and phantasy by the one Sonata, that knowledge will be of service in all others.

Lastly, and this is to art the most important, purely theoretic instruction has an advantage over all others, in that it grants to the pupil freedom of spirit and of decision. It does not hold the work up to him in absolute conception; does not press upon him with the authority of the teacher bending over him; it does not care to rule, but to make the pupil independent, and thus a ruler in his artistic researches. The guiding, instructing word can lead the reader only in so far as it convinces and conquers him. For art cannot be ruled by will of others, feelings of others, and authority over others; but freedom must rule—the whole being must be with it. Therefore man must be free, for the same reason that human worth and worth of a nation are inseparable from the conditions of freedom. Only in this sense does this little book wish to go out. It does not presume to make rules; it offers its contents only as guide and inspiration to individual observations and reflections. Thereby it hopes to bring a twofold release—freedom from foreign authority and release from the bonds of subjectiveness with its moods and caprice. For the true sense of freedom requires that man shall be free through his own reason, released from the network of darkness and of blind impetus and volatility.

It is true that simply theoretic instruction carries with it an impediment by no means to be overlooked. Its revelations, however thoughtful and comprehensive they may be, have only one means of expression—namely, the word. And words do not penetrate into the vitality of a work of art. It has been proven to be absolutely impossible to make known in words the fine vein-work of the stream of life which in reality is ever changing—the constant modulation of accents, the various colorings of expression, in short, the real soul-life of the composition. However, this is by no means intended or desirable. The work of art must not be delivered over, but it must be illumined out of its inner self; it must not be made palatable for the performer; but the spirit of the interpreter should be elevated to it, and made strong enough to accept it. And this can be accomplished by verbal instruction.

PREPARATION.

It is self-evident that the study of Beethoven cannot be undertaken without considerable preparation. It is essential that
the player be above all things a musician, both technically and
through mental development, before he can undertake these
works. No one could think of using them as a means of becoming a pianist; such a plan would not only be unworthy of the
master, but would be decidedly impracticable, as his works are ∪
entirely artistic; and besides, for the development of general
technique, there is sufficient material provided in the works of
Clementi, Mueller, Cramer, Moscheles, Liszt, and a hundred others. Again, no one who is musically undeveloped would undertake the study unless perhaps he might be urged on by the repu-
tation of the composer; but the gain, in that case, would be very
slight. The important question is: What amount of preparation
must be demanded? And the answer must comprise both technique and spiritual development.

Technique.

Just what degree of technical preparation is essential to
Beethoven may not be so easily determined. While his earliest
works resemble those of Haydn and Mozart, in his later ones
(for example the Sonata Op. 106) he seems to go even beyond
the highest demands which the modern piano school exacts of
technique. Indeed, even in the generally simple passages, we
find here and there unforeseen difficulties which go far beyond
the general demands of the whole (technically speaking); for
example, the A major Sonata Op. 2, or the E minor Op. 90.
These peculiar difficulties are the more noticeable from the
fact that Beethoven seldom or never repeats these technically ∨
important moments in other works, as we have been taught to
expect from almost all other piano composers. To have conquered a passage of Thalberg, and a few of Hummel or Chopin,
is to be well in the way toward the acquisition of all the rest,
while in Beethoven nearly every new sentence brings with it new
technical demands. We ought not to find fault with this, but to
rejoice, for the reason that this peculiarity is the newness and

individuality of all of these works, while so many other composers only shake up the kaleidoscope of their mannerisms and figures in order to appear to conjure a new picture. This system
is best set off in the arrangement of compositions of others,
which are sent out under the name of "arrangements, transcrip-
tions, reminiscences." These melodies, borrowed from operas
and folk songs, are intertwined with the necessary passages, regardless of the lack of inner relationship between them. They
are arbitrarily brought together, and as each transcriber chooses
the passages familiar and pleasing to him, he unconsciously and
unavoidably falls into the habit of repetition. Not so Beethoven. With him the accompanying figure and passage of necessity go forth from the thought of the work, and must therefore
be formed according to the variety of the general content.

The constant appearance of new difficulties has led to the
assertion that only virtuosos are able to perform Beethoven's
works. But it would have been a lamentable circumstance for
him and for us if we had been compelled to wait for these virtuosos, for only two have devoted themselves constantly, and with
earnestness, to the work of presenting Beethoven to the lovers
of art. The one was in Beethoven's own lifetime, Czerny, who
studied and performed the works under the master's own direction; the other is Bülow, who for years has, with virtuosity and
highest intelligence, made Beethoven the center of his musical
representations in crowded concert halls. Apart from these (as
has also been remarked by Schindler), up to the present time
very few concert players and virtuosos have manifested intelligence for Beethoven's works. The very vocation of virtuosos
proves that their aim is to shine technically, hence their greatest
daily efforts are spent in the accomplishment of this, leaving
very little time for other thought. Beethoven, though for a long
time himself a concert player, said of virtuosos that "with·agility
of fingers, intelligence and emotion generally run away from
these gentlemen." He was even of the opinion that increased
mechanism in pianoforte playing would finally banish all truth
of perception from music,* a thought which, uttered in the comparatively innocent epoch of a Ries, a Hummel, and a Moscheles,
rings over into our times with the power of a prophecy. No, we
must not be contented with waiting for virtuosos! As each one
can learn to read and love his Goethe, without awaiting declaim-

---

*Beethoven's letter to F. Ries, July 16, 1823: "To speak frankly, I am no admirer of these
things (Allegri di bravura) as they indulge mechanism too greatly."

ing actors and rhetoricians, so each one, in so far as he is able, ought to play his Beethoven. And if he cannot do it at once, let him call in his more skilful friend to repeatedly play what seems too difficult for him to master. If these performances can be accompanied by discussion and analysis, familiarity with the inner thought must follow, in a measure at least.

Let us then not wait for virtuosity, but let us approach Beethoven as soon as possible. Though we may for the present be obliged to dispense with the technically more difficult works, we need not deprive ourselves of the simpler ones. Indeed, we must undertake this, not only for the purpose of enjoyment, but in order to cultivate early the necessary development. From the spiritual as well as from the technical side, Beethoven's works present the appearance of regular progressive order. One may be able to comprehend the more intelligible works, such as Op. 22, 14, 2, 54, 53, etc., and yet by no means have a conception of the deeper works, such as Op. 7, 28, 27 C-sharp minor, 31 D minor, 90, 109, and 110; nor can he suddenly arrive at this maturity, which must be attained through gradual development, by means of spiritually more accessible works. This gradual approach is what so many neglect — it is not a learning, but a living into the very soul of the works, and demands devotion, complete abandonment, inspiration, and love. If, then, an experienced player were to begin with these works which technically have become simple to him, and through which alone he can approach the spiritually higher ones, he will apparently finish them quickly. They do not arouse and fascinate his love of playing, for he thinks they can be finished as the other things which have heretofore occupied his time. He hastens over them, or else refuses them and forgets his spiritual education; or, rather, is unable to appreciate such works.

It has been mentioned above that Beethoven's works are progressive from a technical standpoint also, a technique which extends from the Haydn-Mozart standpoint into the very latest demands. Let me begin with the four-handed marches, Op. 45; the Bagatelles, Op. 33, and the XXXII Variations in C minor, and the Sonatas, Op. 14, 13, 2, 10, 22, 26, 28, 7, 54, 31, 90, 27, 81, 101, 110, 57, 109, 53, 111, 106 will follow in technically increasing order.

It must not be overlooked that this method of grading them can only be a very general one, because every player displays a different degree and direction of virtuosity. For this reason the works have not been presented fully, and those under one Opus number (for example, Opus 14, 2, 10, 31,) have not even been separated according to their self-evident differences. The essential thing has been to cast away the extravagant demands of technical preparation, and in their place to indicate the means of development within the Beethoven circle. An aspiring pianist will at all events never give up his technical studies.

Spiritual Maturity.

It has been admitted above that a certain amount of spiritual development is essential in order to study Beethoven with success But what degree of development? and who can cultivate the same? Who will be the searcher of hearts in these regions? I think that the pupil rather than the teacher or other guide ought to be first listened to. One who desires to approach Beethoven ought not to be prevented from so doing. He may be deceived; his desire for study may be inspired by external motives only (for example, the splendor of Beethoven's name): However that may be, deception and loss of time are not so detrimental as are discouraging refusals and monitions which destroy individuality and therefore power and confidence in artistic success.

But let us assist him who is needy of advice. And he can be assisted if he is directed to such works which are within his sphere of thought. For also from a spiritual standpoint, as has been said before, Beethoven's works follow upon each other, beginning at the most comprehensible, but by no means to be undervalued, and leading on to the highest.

After the Marches Op. 45, the Bagatelles Op. 33, and the 32 Variations No. 36, the Sonatas Op. 13, 14, 2, 54, 22, 53, 78, might follow in this grade. As a second grade, with interspersing of the Bagatelles Op. 119, and the so-called "Denière pensée," the Sonatas Op. 26, 10, 7, 28, 31, 27, 57, would lead on to grade three, which might comprise Op. 81, 90, 106, 101, 110, 109, 111, besides the Variations Op. 120. Where inclination and desire for mental development would inspire a love of the study of Beethoven, the four-handed "Polonaise Concertante" (the Finale of the Triple concerto Op. 56) would be useful in grade one; to grade two might be added the Septette, the first and second

symphony; and to grade three the symphonies 8, 5, 3, 4, arranged
for four hands,* the fifth might be given to technically accomplished students in the exemplary arrangement of Liszt, for two
hands.

But this grading can, like the technical order mentioned before, only serve as a hint and as a foundation from which every
individuality must assume its own place—no absolute rule can
be given. This has been said in order to acquaint those readers
for whom this has been especially written with the nature of the
book.

---

* Care should be taken not to stray to Hummel's and Czerny's arrangement, in which,
through arbitrary addition of the third and fourth discant octave, the orchestral character of
the tone poem deteriorates into mere piano clatter.

BEETHOVEN'S INSTRUMENT.

WITH whatever degree of preparation we may approach Beethoven, we will constantly encounter passages which require further practice. This can not be otherwise, nor can it be considered a reproach to the school of technique. The great object of technical development is to give to arm, hand and fingers that carriage, flexibility and power which is required for pianoforte playing in general. Methods and exercises with this end in view might be called the elementary technique—it is indispensable. There is, however, a series of studies—they might be called art-aspiring studies—whose aim is, by means of special tone-forms (accompanying-figures, passages, etc.) to develop and enlarge the general facility. This portion of technique is as unlimited as musical form itself, that is evident from the thousand of etudes, which already exist, but which never satisfy the demand, because every individual composer, like Beethoven, of necessity brings forth new tone figures. In Beethoven's Sonata, Op. 90, we find for example, the following accompanying formula:

for the left hand, which according to the superscription of the sentence, must be played "with motion" (Allegro con moto), but at the same time, piano, and, to be sure, with perfect equality of tone. The rendering is not without difficulty, especially in relation to the otherwise universal technical simplicity of the passage. This is only an example, of which we find many, to which the technical preparation has not given sufficient development, and which must be studied in its individual place.*

Some of the Beethoven difficulties arise from the difference of the instruments which we use today, and those which he wrote for. Our better instruments have broader and deeper falling keys, the advantages of which are well known, and not to be discussed here. Beethoven was dependent upon the old Vienna grand, which had light, easy tone and action, but little depth and power. He was therefore not satisfied from this direction. "Streicher, (so states Reichardt, 1809) has departed from the soft, too easily yielding and rebounding roll of the other Vienna instruments, and, at Beethoven's advice and request, has given to his instruments more resistance and plasticity." But also the Streicher instruments fell far short of the measure and deep action of the keys of today.

However great the advantage of the modern instruments (with English mechanism) may be over the old Vienna grand, even for Beethoven's music, it is nevertheless evident that many technical demands were more easily complied with in the old instruments. A particular instance of this, is afforded in this passage

---

*The above figure is one of those which have caused the "Klavier masters" to say of him that he did not write "Klaviermassig,"—he, the highest composer for the pianoforte. To be sure, this difficulty might easily have been avoided. Beethoven might have written thus

and that would have been simple. But where would there have been the transparency of the original figure, where the clear tonality and the flowing of the tenths (B-d, c sharp-e, d-f sharp) and the exhilaration which comes to the player by this very difficulty? Beethoven was not the man to deny the spirit which guided him for the sake of the fingers.

from the Finale of the C major Sonata Op. 53. The octave progressions are to be executed "Prestissimo" as well as pianissimo. Beethoven has written for the right hand, the fingering $\frac{5\,5}{1\,1}$ . . ., for the left $\frac{1\,1}{5\,5}$ . . ., and by means of slurs has determined the legato. This can only be accomplished with a gliding, glissando movement, and is not so difficult on the old instruments, while with ours it seems nearly impossible. It would seem that to carefully fulfill the three conditions, prestissimo, pianissimo, and legato, there would be no other way but to change. We would then play thus

sacrificing the deep bass octaves. I well recognize the dangers of this suggestion, which, for easy-going and less conscientious natures might easily become the signal for further changes. However, this consideration must still not withhold the truth,

without which the passage is uninterpretable, or at least would
compel the percussive effect ("pondré"). Besides, the above
rendering is supported by the approval of Bülow, who, as one of
the greatest players, is an authority in matters of technique.
Finally, I may add with full conviction, that to me at least, after
many years of experience with Beethoven's works, no passage
haspresented itself which was impossible to express; with the
exception, perhaps, of a single figure, used several times. This
figure likewise presents itself in the Finale of the same Sonata in
the first tempo, Allegretto moderato,

which is first to be played "Pianissimo" and then "Fortissimo."
The difficulty lies in the right hand which, at the same time with
the trill, plays the melody, and, further, as we always understand in Beethoven, it must be played with expression. Here it
might be advisable to interrupt the trill during the entrance of
the melody

and to play it so that the tones which fall together with the trill
in the original, shall not be pointed or bitten off, but shall stand
forth smooth and quiet. A similar thing (only for one measure)
occurs in the so-called Menuett of the D major Sonata Op. 10,
and perhaps also in other passages. Here again the exact rendering must have been less difficult on instruments of older
construction, but the omission of single trill tones can hardly
be perceived, especially in rolling, quick execution. Opposed
to all these little difficulties, which originate partially in the
construction of the new instrument, stands nevertheless unques-
tionably the avantage which these have over the others, even
for Beethoven. Only one defect is seen in most of them, and
that might easily be remedied. They have but one movement
of the soft pedal which brings the hammer from three strings
upon two, but not however, an additional one (through deeper
pressing of the same pedal) which brings it upon one string.
The latter brings about an entirely peculiar tone character, especially in the deeper tones, and is by no means a mere assistance
for pianissimo playing. Beethoven has depended upon this in
various ones of his deepest passages, for example, in the Sonata
Op. 106, and has carefully written " unacorde," "duendo," "tutte
corde." This double movement upon the different strings, so
indispensable to certain tone effects, is nevertheless easily combined with the modern construction of the instrument, and can
even be added without difficulty to finished pianos. This
arrangement has no defect as to durability. Formerly I played
for years an English grand built for Prince Louis (therefore
before 1806) and now I have had in my possession for more than
twenty years an excellent Breitkopf & Häertel grand, of English
mechanism, both with double soft pedal movement and most
desirable durability. It is essential to demand this arrangement
assiduously, from piano manufacturers, and to treat with greater
care the single string, which, to be sure, is more easily brought
out of tune.

BEETHOVEN'S FINGERING.

THE *technique* of pianoforte playing has attained, up to Beethoven, and since his time, a high degree of perfection. To undervalue the advantages which reach beyond Beethoven's standpoint would certainly be mistaken appreciation,— we must not strive after his outward means, but after his purpose, and must use the best means available.

Let us first consider his fingering. We cannot undertake here to thoroughly treat this subject; that, so far as necessary, must have preceded the study of Beethoven, in the technical preparation. We will only touch those points which are particularly important for the representation of his works, and those only in so far as they are indispensable.

It is well known that there are few absolute rules for fingering,—perhaps none at all,—because many different ends may be decisive. The most important is availability in general; next in order comes ease and certainty; then lightness and fluency of melody; then furthering of the particular expression; lastly even the construction of the hand of each individual player requires attention, as that which may be difficult or impossible for one hand may be simple for another. There may therefore be more than one fingering for the same sentence, without giving one or the other the preference. It is, however, advisable that each one decide in favor of some fingering, because otherwise there is much time and energy wasted, and one fingering destroys steadiness in the other.*

Finally, we may recognize that simplicity and proper sequence of fingering simplifies the practice; that we must use, in the same motive, as far as possible the same succession of fingers; that we must have for each successive key that finger available which is most convenient for it,—and whatever other general and practical rules there may be. Even beside the well-known finger order for the major scale, there are others more favorable for special passages. Indeed, transference of the same finger (especially the second) from one key to the following may seem desirable, when it becomes necessary, in order to feelingly indi-

---

* This remark is not unnecessary. One of our most excellent teachers and players has, especially in Beethoven, the habit of giving his pupils as many as four different fingerings which they are to practice.

vidualize the tones at once with certainty and the finest gradations of intensity or expressiveness.*

Once for all, let it be distinctly understood that these and
other departures are not advantageous to a pianist whose insight
and skill in fingering are not yet firmly determined. But players
of this class are not yet ripe for Beethoven—at least not for
those works which make departures of such a character necessary.

If such variations are admissible for every other composition,
how much more so must they be for Beethoven's tone poems,
which consist throughout of the finest sentiment, and are determined by the most manifold contents! Here again the fingering,
as the means for success and expression, must be an important
consideration at every new attempt,—the more so, as Beethoven
undoubtedly followed a deeper impetus than technical consideration; and when he, at the close of a composition, attempted to
simplify things by adding fingering, he more often fell short, or
at least fell far behind, the clear insight into sequence of fingers.
In such cases we would be acting in opposition to the thought of
the master were we to resort to his means instead of better ones.

Now for a few examples:

1. One-voiced Figures.

In the A-major Sonata, Op. 2, we find the following figure
progressing downwards at A and upwards at B:

---

*An example of this may be found on page 36, in the illustration from the D-minor Sonata.
See the fingering in brackets of the *d* chord, first measure.—TRANS.

The tempo is *Allegro vivace*. Whether or not the indicated fingering was added by Beethoven himself is not known. The execution is, as it stands, very difficult, and for small hands hardly possible. Czery* calls the left hand to assistance and

thereby obviates the difficulty entirely. To Beethoven himself this manner of playing must have been known; he has written, for example, in the first movement of the B-flat major Sonata, Op. 106 (page 8 of the original edition by Artaria), thus (A),

instead of as at B, in order to bring out the passage (*Allegro* and *piano*) with greater certainty and lightness. He requires the same manner of playing in the first movement of the A-flat major Sonata, Op. 110 (*Moderato*, measure 12 of the original edition of Schlesinger). At first, however, he writes thus for the right hand,

while he gives the left hand rests. The passage is nevertheless very readily played in this manner. It stands out lighter and with better quality (it is marked *piano* and *leggiermente*) when

* Klavierschule, Part 4.

we allow the left hand to share it, as above indicated; and
thus Beethoven has himself further on written at least once.
Perhaps this manner of indicating, which is so much more satisfactory to the player, may have been too cumbersome for him,
or he may have thought of the *technique* only this once.

This alternate use of the hands seems desirable even in less
difficult figures—providing it adds to the spiritual interpretation.
In the D-minor Sonata, Op. 31, the second part of the first movement begins with these arpeggios,

which (as the rests in the bass indicate) seem to be intended for
the right hand, and present no technical difficulties to the player
who is fully prepared for this Sonata. Nevertheless, if the hands
were to relieve each other, as is indicated above (the lower fingering is for the left, the upper for the right hand) such movement would be favorable to a finer rendering. Here also the
movement of the second finger (page 33) seems applicable to
bringing the last tones out with finest feeling.

But also for the exact opposite expression, this manner of
rendering may be useful. In the first movement of the F-minor
Sonata, Op. 57, from a continued pianissimo, the following arpeggio figure bursts forth *forte* (measure 14):

According to the thought and character of the movement, this must stand forth particularly strong and striking. The rendering is not difficult, even in the tempo *allegro assai*, and *forte*. However, the necessary steady power would be supported by the use of both hands, each one striking with the third finger, or else with regular fingering.

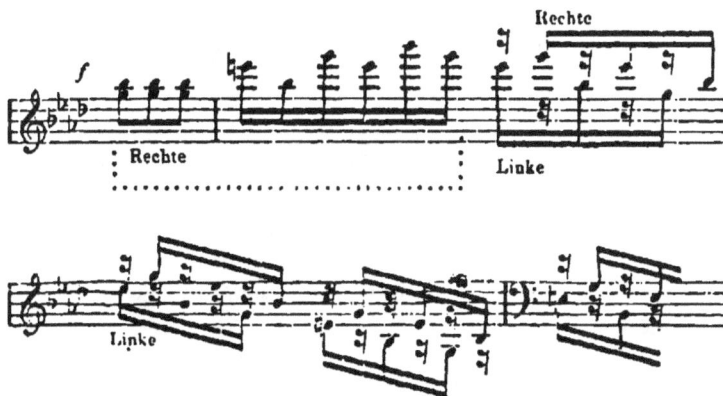

Players for whom this form of representation is not fluent, will exert their utmost strength in single-handed performance.

A trifle is yet to be considered here at the close of these propositions, the advisability of which is not entirely agreed upon; it is the progression in fourths, of the right hand, in the trio of the F-minor Sonata, Op. 2. Beethoven (or an unknown person for him) has fingered this passage thus:

Czerny, to whom this fingering may have seemed without foundation, has offered the following:

$$
\begin{array}{llll}
454 & 545454 & 554543 & 4543454 \\
121 & 212121 & 212121 & 2121212
\end{array}
$$

and Bülow (in oral intercourse) has suggested a more simple sequence, thus:

$$
\begin{array}{llll}
454 & 545454 & 545454 & 5454545 \\
121 & 212121 & 212121 & 2121212
\end{array}
$$

If we look at the beginning of the sentence, we perceive that it begins two-voiced, in thirds; and that the voice which forms the fourths enters later on.

It would not be at variance with the character of the composition to refer to the left hand the two voices proceeding in thirds, as belonging together and forming a foundation—perhaps with this fingering:

and to yield the upper voice as the melodic one to the right hand. For small hands this division and fingering (next to von Bülow's fingering for the progression of fourths) seems most acceptable. Beethoven has himself suggested it, in the Finale of the A-major Sonata, Op. 101 (page 16 of the original edition of Steiner), for three measures, and has thereby supplied the annotation for this Sonata, Op. 2.

Two or More Voices in One Hand.

As soon as two or more voices need to be expressed with one hand, the demand for departure from the fundamental rules of fingering becomes greater,—or, rather, new rules are required which are as authoritative as the simpler ones intended only for one-voiced passages in one hand. The playing of one-voiced sentences is without doubt easier; therefore, wherever it is possible, we must relieve the hand which carries the chief melody from all other difficulties. A little example of this is given in the Adagio of the F-minor Sonata, Op. 2. Beethoven has written measure 2 and 3 as at A — —

placing rests for the left hand, and therefore assigning the notes *c, b, b-flat* to the right hand. Although the rendering of this is very simple, yet the transferring of the three tones to the left hand, as is shown at B, would be preferable, because the right hand gains freedom for the most delicate intonation of the melody.

Now for a few examples for the simultaneous utterance, by means of one hand, of two or more tones or voices, which may serve as models for like passages.

In the first movement of the A-major Sonata, Op. 2, the second part closes as follows:

piano and *pianissimo.* Nothing seems more suitable than to touch the two keys *d* and *c* with the thumb of the right hand, because otherwise the outer tones of the upper and lower voices must be sprung upon, which would give a feeling of unrest and hardness to the touch.

In the Finale of the D-major Sonata, Op. 28 (original edition by Haslinger, page 18), the left hand has the following passage (A):

occurring four times, and *fortissimo*. It is clear that the eighths must be taken with the fingers 4 3 2, therefore the second finger must spring from *d* to *c*, and, finally, *c-sharp f* must be taken with the fingers 4 and 2. If we wished, furthermore, to shorten the tone *a* (as shown at B), a movement which would seem contrary to Beethoven's direction and intention, the little finger would be obliged to jump from *a* to *b*, and the inconvenient movement 4 2 from *c-sharp* to *f* would still take place.

In the closing sentence of the C-major Sonata the left hand must be conducted thus:

the little finger plays successive white keys, also moves from white to black keys, and (*a b-flat*) the thumb likewise passes over two white keys, *a b*, and also from black to white, *b-flat c*.

In the Adagio of the B-flat major Sonata, Op. 22, measure 39,

the little finger is obliged to carry the entire upper voice. This manner of playing is not absolutely necessary, since we might use 4 4 5 4; however, it is more desirable than the apparently more regular changing of fingers, and is more adapted to giving each tone of the little melody the emphasis due to it.

In the first movement of the D-major Sonata, Op. 28, measure 48,

the thumb is to be moved from *f-sharp* to *e;* the fifth finger is to be slipped under the fourth.

In the Finale of the A-major Sonata, Op. 101 (page 14 in the original edition by Steiner), there is a passage for the right hand which cannot well be rendered otherwise than thus:

Likewise for the left hand, thus:

The right hand requires a similar treatment in the following passage, A, from the same movement (page 13, Steiner edition):

The trill might be interrupted, as is shown at B.

Finally, our attention must be directed toward those passages in which, in the leading through of several voices, one of them passes from one hand into the other, either of necessity or in favor of expressive utterance. An example of this presents itself in the Scherzo of the third Sonata, Op. 2,

where the second voice is introduced by the left hand and then taken up by the right hand, in order that the former may become free for introducing the third voice.

A second example of this presents itself in the Finale of the B-flat major Sonata, Op. 106 (page 44 of the original edition), at the transition into G-flat major:

and still a third in A-flat major (page 46),

which immediately repeats itself. The necessity is obvious at once. Less comprehensible is the changing hands in the twenty-fourth variation of the 33 Variations, Op. 120. In this exqui-sitely delicate variation, the entrance of alto, soprano, and bass (it is a little *fugato*) is plainly perceptible; not so the entrance of the tenor, among the other voices, in the first measure given be-low:

In order not to blur the voices and to allow the tenor to enter clearly, the left hand must venture upon the spring *c–g*, right into the midst of the other hand. The second measure given above is simpler.

THE BEETHOVEN TECHNIQUE.

HOWEVER great the progress of the new *technique* may be, nevertheless, in accordance with the character of modern compositions — especially those of concert and *salon* composers — it has been guilty of a certain one-sidedness.

Naturally the first aim of *technique* is to give to hands and fingers the highest attainable degree of velocity, certainty, lightness, and power — full control over the keyboard. To this end all elementary exercises and all études are directed. This development, thoroughly advisable in the first period of pianoforte playing, and in the attainment of virtuosity, has, of necessity, led toward treating the hand with the fingers more as a whole, as a single organ. Brilliancy and mastery on the part of the player require, in order to manifest themselves, extensively developed runs and arpeggios; the hand must be led over several octaves, and the fingers must carry on the play of figures in extended passages. Études and concertos are based upon this; also the so-called *salon* pieces. All this is accomplished exclusively, or most perceptibly, through masses of tones, each of which, through equality of rendering, is melted into a whole.

That this manner of playing is applicable also to Beethoven, is self-evident; the long passages in the first movement of the B-flat major Sonata, Op. 106, in the trio of the A-flat major Sonata, Op. 110, in the C-major Sonata, Op. 53, and many others, may serve as examples. More noteworthy (because more often neglected, and at times more difficult to execute) are certain forms of accompaniment. The B-flat major Trio, Op. 97, begins with this accompaniment:

which must be rendered with absolute evenness of touch and
power or, in measure 3, with crescendo. This is not so easy, as
the little finger must keep equal pace with the thumb and two
middle fingers.

In the Finale of the F-minor Sonata, Op. 2, the triplet accompaniment in the left hand must be played with absolute equality;
it forms, as it were, the ground work upon which the passionate
figures of the melody develop themselves. However, in the
closing theme this is changed: the melody moves for twice-
eight measures, in quiet, grand resignation above the continuing
accompaniment,

in which the passionate storm of the deeply agitated soul is still
perceptible. This accompaniment must be played with the
utmost uniformity of movement and intonation (no tone rising
above the other); at the same time it must begin *pp*, and with
absolute evenness swell to a *fortissimo* up to measure 6, and end
as follows: *

* The single mark (—) means a simple emphasis, two and three marks (= and ≡) greater degrees of intensity.

and the following eight measures have the same treatment

In the Trio (marked minor) of the E-flat major Sonata, Op. 7, both hands have the following figure:

This again must be played with most perfect equality, with a gentle crescendo to the first tone of the third measure, then diminuendo, in like manner repeated, and then according to the indications given by Beethoven himself. The second part explains itself; the entire sentence might be interpreted by the words of the poet—

> 'Mid rustling winds
> In quiet night.

The melody here should be as undefined as the inarticulate rustle of winds. The melody lies in the simultaneous sounding together of the tones; these tone masses

are at the same time the first four harmonies and the first four
moments of the melody. So much will serve as an example
(though by no means an exhaustive one) of the even play of the
hands and fingers toward which the newer *technique* is principally
directed. In Beethoven,. however, we meet entirely different
demands, to the satisfying of which this *technique* does not lead;
on the contrary, it seems even to a certain extent to lead away.
In Beethoven (likewise in Bach, often in Mozart, and in every
poetic and deep composer) it becomes necessary every moment
that one hand — yea, even one or more fingers in the same hand
—should be liberated and made independent in order to bring
about a certain effect. The former — i. e., the independence of
one hand over another — is simple. A stronger intonation of a
melody in one hand, as compared with the accompaniment in
the other, is demanded, at any rate, by every teacher, and is
accomplished by every player. The demand (taking for granted
the skill of each hand for that which is under consideration) is
generally simple, but occasionally requires *finesse* of understanding and interpretation. In the first movement of the G-major
Sonata, Op. 14, for example, the speaking melody

requires to be played with expression, with gradual swelling of
the four or five *d*'s, and a decreasing close; the accompaniment,
on the other hand, must be subdued and must flow evenly onward, with a barely perceptible emphasis on the first and fifth sixteenth. The difficulty, if there is any, lies in the third measure,
in the five repeated *d*'s, which must increase in breadth very

gently, while the left hand in similar movement does not change. It is a peculiar thing that now and then it seems to be more in accordance with the idea to think the melody in one hand quite differently from that which is played, simultaneously with the other. An example of this is to be found at the beginning of the F-minor Sonata, Op. 57. Both hands have the same melody

until near the end of the passage, and this melody must be rendered *legato* and *pp*. Whoever has penetrated into the mysterious, spectral nature of this poem will comply with the suggestion of playing the deeper voice still more softly than the higher one; it is, as it were, the shadow of a shadow.

If, however, the same hand must supply different demands, the fingers must, of necessity, be prepared therefor; not only in the sense that each finger must be able to do as much as every other (so that, for example, the little finger may be able to use equal power with the third), but even that one finger may be sustaining a melodic tone, while the other subordinates itself; or that one part of the hand may be playing *staccato*, while the other is playing *legato*. This is a point which is very much neglected in the newer *technique*, and only then comes into the foreground when a certain composition requires it. In order to become convinced of the necessity of this, analyze sentences of this kind, as to their various sets of voices, without regard to means of playing, or difficulties, and make clear to yourself what the contents really are. When this is thoroughly mastered, the means of outward expression will comply with the demands.

These means of expression depend, of course. upon the complete control of every finger and upon the constant thought and watchfulness over the use of them. In delicate passages the keys must not be struck, but must be touched with feeling,—the tenderest feeling. In intense passages, on the contrary, the fingers must strike the keys with percussive power. The hand must come to the assistance of the fingers. If the wrist is raised, all the fingers will respond with increased intensity, on account of the more steep downward stroke thus produced. The middle fingers are especially assisted by this. If the wrist is lowered, the fingers will fall straighter, and the power of the hand will be lessened. If the hand is bent slightly outward, its power favors the little finger; if bent inward, the thumb is aided. Even a slight bending of the little finger in the upper joint may assist those who are able to accomplish this, for passages which require a stretched-out and therefore flat position of the hand, and which may still require a bringing out of those tones which fall to the little finger. It is comprehensible that these departures from the normal balance of the hand must be used sparingly, and only by players whose *technique* is already established.

Occasionally, when no other means are available, it even becomes necessary to move the important tones almost imperceptibly forward or backward; or perhaps to give them in strict time, and imperceptibly to touch the others a little after. This last expedient should, however, be used very conscientiously, and only in case of absolute necessity. As soon as it becomes at all perceptible, it undermines, so to speak, the entire body of tone, and makes it more or less fragile.

In order to illustrate by simple examples, how many different kinds of touch are necessary in the simultaneous working of the fingers, I first call attention to the beginning of the Andante from the G-major Sonata, Op. 14. At A

the individual chords are separated from each other by rests and *staccato* marks; at B they are to be bound together. The characteristic is, that in both cases the tones of the melody fall together, stroke for stroke, with those of the accompaniment. The very same thing is seen in the first measures of the C-major Sonata, Op. 53,

and repeats itself in this passage, as also in other places.   In all instances of this kind, the most accurate simultaneous sounding together of the tones is essential, while at the same time a slight emphasis of the melodic tones is required.

A similar case, a little more difficult to render, is found in the Fantasie-Sonata, E-flat major, Op. 27.   Here also,

in addition to the melody, a part of the accompaniment (three and two tones) falls to the right hand.   All tones falling on the same pulse must come accurately together; but at the same time the melody must be intoned clearly and expressively above the accompanying tone-mass.   It must not be supposed by the player, that simply the longer holding of the melodic tones will distinguish them from the accompaniment, but they must be made clear through stronger intonation (again with moderation). In the eighths, 1, 3, 5, and 8 of the first, and 1, 2, 3, 4, 5, and 7 of the second measure, every melodic tone must be heard above the accompanying mass.

A similar rendering is required for the melody when it meets, in the same hand, with a florid accompaniment, as in this instance

of the C-sharp minor Sonata, Op. 27, where after a little prelude of the accompanying voices, the melody enters and is carried far onward. The coming together of the tones in the right hand must be brought about very evenly,—but they must not be uttered with the same intensity (as though $\begin{cases} \textit{g-sharp } \overline{a} \\ \textit{g-sharp a,} \end{cases}$ were to be played as octaves); rather with emphasis of the melodic tones. The majority of players are contented with even playing and even strength for both tones; but thereby the melody is drawn down into the sphere of the accompaniment.

But again, the manner of playing, so common to modern virtuosos, which brings out—one might say hammers out—the melodic tones with equal emphasis, cannot suffice. Every melody (with very rare exceptions) demands the elastic touch which is peculiar to the feeling and sentiment; it requires the change from principal to subordinate moments, from greater to lesser intensity, in which sympathy of expression and intelligence is manifested. This must take place in every melody; consequently, also, in those in which other tones enter in the same hand.

Similar passages are found in the Sonata Pathétique, and frequently in other places. I will give only one more illustration from the second movement of the E-minor Sonata, Op. 90:

The melody lies in the upper voice (*a, g-sharp, g-sharp, f-sharp,* etc.), and is supported by the accompanying voices, running evenly on at the same time. Between the pairs of voices, the uppermost and lowermost, two middle voices lead through the figure of sixteenths. This figure must be subdued; it must pass through with exceeding softness and evenness, like a whisper, while the melody, together with the nearest related voices, must be heard fuller, and must be made expressive with suitable accentuation. To emphasize this upper voice over its adjoining voices would seem arbitrary; and the effect of the whole would be weakened rather than strengthened by a super-abundance of gradations of color.

At all events, we should not go too far in gradations of tone, lest fluency and unity of the whole suffer thereby.

BEETHOVEN'S MELODY.

HAVING reviewed the means, we now approach the main subject, namely, the interpretation of the Beethoven works. Who could here be a better instructor than Beethoven himself? And though we can no longer listen to his playing, nevertheless earwitnesses are not wanting who can enlighten us as to his manner of expression.

Let us first consider the noble old K. F. Reichardt.* He speaks of an Academie (concert) given by Beethoven in 1808, in which the master performed the G-major Concerto, Op. 58. "The Adagio," so relates Reichardt, "a masterpiece of beautifully developed song, he fairly sung on his instrument, with a deep melancholy feeling which seemed to penetrate me also." Reichardt was particularly, and above all others, capable of appreciating this tone quality, for he had not only learned from the great master Gluck, in Italy, what tone singing is, but he had himself practiced it with delight. In Beethoven's Adagio he again perceived this song, this melting together of soul emotions, with the wave-like motion, pliability, and facility of the sympathetic voice. Here the soul never becomes rigid; it constantly bubbles up and quiets itself amid the change of pressing on and calming, in which the mood forms itself and makes itself manifest.

A second earwitness appears to explain still further the suggestion made by Reichardt. Schindler, a pupil, and for many years a friend of the master, says of his playing, " It was the plainest, most comprehensive declamation which can be studied with the same degree of potency, perhaps only in his works. This is especially true of the Pathétique; what this work became in his hands was so remarkable that one needed to have heard and reheard it, in order to recognize the same well-known work."

When Schindler compares Beethoven's performance to a finished declamation, therefore to a conscious language of words, he indicates thereby that beyond the representation of indeterminate sense and soul agitations (of which Reichardt has

* For further information see " Beethoven, Life and Works," 3d Ed., II, page 104 f.

spoken) an entirely assured spirit had become master of all these emotions. The thought, the excited, mysterious fluctuations of the soul, were conditions and foundations; the clearly comprehending, determined, and determining spirit was the builder and finisher.

Yet another word of Schindler's (which I too, independently of him, have spoken) must be emphasized. He says that this Beethovenian declamation can be studied *perhaps* only in his works. Let us take Sebastian Bach, and Gluck, and selections from other masters, and the "perhaps" will be changed into an "absolutely"; especially when pianoforte music is under consideration. Nearly all pianoforte compositions lack the earnestness of a steady temperament, and also, more particularly, that penetrative insight which is directed toward the ideal and rests there. They lack that yielding and abandonment to the one determining idea which did not come into complete existence until called there by Beethoven's creations. This refers to his works as a whole, but is true even of the *melody* alone, if indeed that term may be used to designate the voice which particularly, and above all other voices, carries the main contents of the whole within itself.

The Beethoven melody is radically different from the majority of other melodies. There is a certain external characteristic which can be tested before going deeper into the contents. Indeed it is more comprehensive, in general, than other melodies, therefore must contain more and have more to say. This conclusion could only be disputed, if the contents were found to be trivial, or if we could discover unnecessary repetitions and interpolations. This, however, is never the case, and the very opposite can be proven. Beethoven's manner of speech is seen to be conclusive throughout, and at the same time—rather for that very reason—is penetrative. A few examples will show this.

The principal theme of the first Allegro of the Pathétique

has eight measures of unbroken, progressive song, and repeats itself with a far leading transition in measure 8 of the repetition. The tonic progression rises actively for two octaves, but sinks (3) in quieter movement for one octave. Section one (1) is

repeated (at 2); but it is not a mere repetition, but a progression
into the higher octave, and the phrasing becomes more marked,
through the syncopated form.

The E-minor Sonata, Op. 90, builds its thesis, up to the antithesis, into a decidedly complete period,

di - mi - nu - en - dò

which repeats itself four times (1 to 4). The antithesis also
repeats its first section (5 and 6), and then moves in one progression to the close. Thus is formed a melody of

$$2 + 2 + 2 + 2 \text{ and } 2 + 2 + 4,$$

sixteen measures in all. However, the melody is not yet brought
to a close. The last eight of the above-named measures have
somewhat improperly been called the antithesis, in order to designate the importance of these eight measures. Upon more
careful observation, these sixteen measures taken together prove
to be the thesis; and the antithesis follows in measure 17, and,
attached to section one, but reaching further, brings with it a
subject of four measures, with its repetition, which again under-
goes an alteration.

Here we find, then, one single melody of twenty-four measures, the song register of which now and then extends from *e* to *e̅*.
There seems nowhere a possibility of an earlier close; everywhere there is a desire to move on. Throughout, a feeling of conclusiveness is manifest. The first motive appears six times; one
sentence constantly determines the other; 1 leads to 4, and to
the motive of the antithesis which appears in measure 17. Nowhere do we find simply repetition; every return is a transformation and a progressive forward motion.

The same characteristics of conclusiveness and of restless pressing forward are shown in the Largo of the D-major Sonata, Op. 10, in the entire first subject of the D-minor Sonata, Op. 31, and in the Adagio of the B-flat major sonata, Op. 106. Everywhere, in fact, with exception of a few small works, we find these peculiarities which are indicative of the absorption out of which the master created. Each individual melody is a most important moment of the life of its creator. They are not thoughts or inspirations strung together, for the soul pours out its contents in an uninterrupted current (Reichardt); the spirit, conclusive and clearly defined, strides on from one idea to the following ones, onward toward its destination, which it finally attains (Schindler).

How, then, shall the player treat these melodies? First of all, he must adhere to the conviction that there is nothing useless or empty, that every tone is called forth and permeated by the conscious spirit of the tone poet; that therefore each tone must be felt by the player also, and must be reproduced in soulful manner. In order to convince oneself of this by an opposite, examine Hummel's Adagios, and observe the gayly festooned fiorituri which the finger-gnome of the virtuoso has placed in them, strewing them in among dignified melodies.

Secondly, the player must not confine himself to single moments, and the searching out of them; he must press on to the inner relationship, and reveal the relation of each moment to the whole, and, in this place, its individual importance. Indeed, he must observe how the same phrase at its repetition augments its significance, or is otherwise changed. In the above-cited passage of the E-minor Sonata these frequently very fine and half-concealed changes may be traced even in Beethoven's text, although he may not be accurate in his notation. Besides, notations (page 14) cannot represent the subject exhaustively. In this melody, in the first part and its repetitions (2, 3, 4), pitch character of tone, and key change constantly. Even the character of the upbeat varies; at 1 and 3 it is marked as ♪ ⅋, at 2 and 4 as ♪. The very nicety and apparent unimportance of this distinction (the passage is to be played con moto) testifies of the fineness and sharp definiteness with which the master created. What means, then, are at the service of the player for such representation?

To answer this, let us realize what takes place in agitated soul life. There we nowhere find indifference or coldness, nowhere a standing still or letting go; for indeed movement and change rule throughout — movement of the restless and quieting emotions, and change of the determined will, either letting go of its tension or being strengthened within itself.

These emotions reflect themselves in the movement or temporal relationship of the tones, and in the wave play of the various degrees of intensity, which, all together, must lie as clearly before the spirit of the player as the keys do before his eye, or rather before his play instinct.

Of the movement, let only one thing be remarked here. If this is indicated by tempo marking and through metric valuation (and it will be seen that both indications do not rule immutably), the player will still find opportunity enough in the varied gradations of staccato and legato playing, to prolong or shorten the duration of single tones. Legato playing, even though carried on in strict time, constantly has the effect of lingering, while staccato has a tendency to a pressing forward. More important observations will follow later.

Establishing the intensity depends first of all upon the sentiment of the tone picture in general. It is self-evident that a tender or light-spirited composition — as for example the F-minor Sonata, Op. 2, or the G-major Sonata, Op. 14 — cannot possibly be raised to the same intensity as would be suitable for the F-minor Sonata, Op. 57, or the B-flat major Sonata, Op. 106. Even the annotations *f* and *ff* have an entirely different significance in the former from what they have in the latter. It is, then, particularly the measurement of the degrees of intensity which seems to give expression to the rhythmic accents, thereby forming the structure of the whole tone composition and making it intelligible. Without this intonation, the tone body would run, as it were, into an indistinct and shapeless mass.

But rhythmic construction, on the other hand, is by no means contained in metric progression alone, so that the well-known rules would suffice, — namely, that we are to emphasize the first pulse, or in composite measure (⁴⁄₄, ⁶⁄₈, etc.) the primary and secondary accent (in ⁶⁄₈ the first and fourth, in ⁴⁄₄ the first and third), and that the primary must be more emphatic than the secondary. A single measure is not always a closed whole; on the contrary, it seldom is complete. Indeed, it requires two or more measures to form a complete unit, — a section, — thesis and antithesis, principal and counter themes, etc. These members must through intonation be made comprehensible beyond the construction of the individual measure. Of other means of expression we cannot speak now.

Whoever understands composition must have full insight into this tone formation; however, it is not difficult for the less instructed to recognize it. Let us look back once more at the last illustration (from the F.-minor Sonata). The four sections, of two measures each, are comprehensively determined and separated by rests. Beethoven has designated them, not only through the annotation of *f* for sections one and three, and *p* for sections two and four, but also by the determined manner of playing; the upbeat for the *forte* passage is to be played staccato (♪ ♩), therefore more sharply, while that of the *piano* section is to be dwelt upon (♩), therefore is to be made more tender. The closing tones are formed in like manner. The change of intonation and intensity might be marked thus,

only that section 3 as a whole is to be more marked than section 1, and that 4 should be less subdued than 2. The following sections

are to be *piano* (the *p* of section 4 continues) and are to be legato, and therefore are subject to softer playing. They are therefore, according to directions, less sharply formed. However, the coupling of measures continues, and finds expression in the shortening of the tones marked with †, which, according to the phrasing, lose a trifle of their value (♪ ♩ or ♪ ♩). Each section begins with tender intonation, and closes *diminuendo*, as is indicated in the last. Only the last three tones of the last section

may be emphasized, and are (according to Beethoven's directions) to be retarded at the same time, in order to define more
distinctly the close of the long thesis and to lead to the antithesis.

Casually another means has become visible, for illustrating
the building up of the members, and for releasing one section
from another: that is, making a pause by shortening the end
tone. In the first sections, Beethoven has indicated these pauses
(cæsuras) through rests; in the following ones they are somewhat pointed out through phrase marks; but even without annotations, they must be observed. The theme of the first sentence
of the Pathétique must therefore, in its first half, be played thus,

although Beethoven (and justly too, for he could, and had
to depend upon the intelligence of the player) has annotated
the closing tone of the first section (the first of the third measure) as a quarter note. Now and then the construction lies
hidden deeper, as for instance in the Adagio of the large B-flat
major Sonata, Op. 106,

where, with exception of the first measure, unmistakable sections
of 4 and 4, then 2 and 2 measures (marked ††) stand forth; but
also still smaller forms (marked †) might be made more distinct
by shortening or by decreasing the vibration. Two dangers
must here be guarded against. Firstly, let no one attempt
to carry into the compositions the circumlocuitous annotations
which serve here only for exemplification, and which still are
inadequate for defining expression; secondly, let no one sup-
pose that these rhythmic accents, this melodic construction,
was the only determining force in the composer. He has followed the changing conditions of his soul; as his was a poetic

one, it was under the sway of order,—that is, the ordered rhythm which is the fundamental characteristic of all intelligent beings. Both qualities lived and worked inseparably in the composer.

Intensity marks have proved themselves serviceable to the sense of the composition as a whole, and to the change of the rhythmic accents. They are useful also to those moments of feeling, which, entirely independent of the rhythm,--one might say, incalculable,—now press on, occasionally with violence, now hide and extinguish themselves, as though attempting to hie away unobserved. For these manifestations, rising immediately from the emotions, and constantly belonging to the particular sentiment of the passage, there can be no general law. Only one observation will often be useful—often, but not always. In most cases, passages leading upward will require an intensifying of power, and descending ones a diminishing of the same. For rising upward in the realm of tone, intensification of power and movement are relative, as it were, synonymous manifestations of a more intense soul movement; and so a descent in the realm of tone, a decrease of power and movement, are indicative of a quieting of the soul emotion. In such a manner, for example, the first passage of the Pathétique Sonata might be played. After the first tone, c, which, as strong pulse, and because of its duration, requires emphasis, the tone series, $\bar{e} \mid f,\ g,\ \bar{a}\text{-}flat,\ \bar{b} \mid \bar{c}$, must be intensified. The syncopation must receive emphasis because it is a repetition of the first c, and from here there must be another crescendo up to the highest $\bar{c}$. In order, however, that amid a double intensification the emphasis of the first c may not be lost, every swell must begin with a weaker intensity than the preceding c received. The sentence ought to be marked thus:

but the second part (from $\bar{c}$) would need to begin and close with a greater degree of intensity than the first; and out of every increasing tone series the strong pulses ($\bar{f}$ and $\bar{f}$) would need to be brought out with a slight emphasis.*

---

* This is a verification of the assertion of page 14 in regard to the inadequacy of written rules for expression. Signs upon signs are heaped upon each other in the score, and yet by no means all is indicated which must be observed in execution.

According to the same law (if indeed a general advice which admits of a hundred exceptions may be so called), the first theme of the small F-minor Sonata (A)

would be played with a crescendo to $\bar{a}$-*flat* (with slight stress upon the first *f*), and then diminuendo.   The side theme (B) would be played with a decrescendo, with emphasis upon the first *e-flat* and the last *f-flat*.

However, as has been remarked before, the here elucidative law is by no means to be carried out without exceptions.   An important consideration, often in opposition to this, is the limited vibratory power of the highest tones.   If the attempt is made to intensify this power beyond the capacity of the string, the click of the hammer is more perceptible than the tone. Other means, however, will present themselves where intensification of the vibrating power is not feasible.

BEETHOVEN'S ACCOMPANIMENT.

THE separation of melody and accompaniment (as, for ab-
breviation, at present all will be called which is not a principal voice) is entirely inconsistent with the idea of art.
To the composer, the melody does not appear alone—as a fore-
runner to the accompaniment, to be made later on; but both
appear simultaneously to the spirit of the tone poet. If now
and then only single moments of that whole which is being created, rise up in the spiritual conception, they are as likely to
belong to the accompaniment as to the principal voice. In the
Finale of the. F-minor Sonata, Op. 57, the stormy accompanying figure was created first.

The separation of melody and harmony is only undertaken
for the sake of a more careful investigation; just as the knife of
the anatomist separates the members which belong together, in
order to show forth more thoroughly their construction and relationship. The result of the investigation must be comprehension of the relationships, of the interworkings, and of life.

That which above was called, in a general way, accompaniment, comprises within itself three different formations. First,
actual accompaniment, a tone mass which has no specific, marked
contents, but which obviously is determined only for the service
of the principal voice, in order to carry it and support it. In the
example (page 45) of the B-flat major Trio, for instance, the
melody and actual accompaniment stand out from each other
clearly defined. Secondly, there is distinguishable from this pure
accompaniment a counter-voice, or a union of several counter-
voices which have peculiarly stamped contents which they subordinate, however, to an undeniably ruling principal voice. Such
is the case in the large F-minor Sonata. Finally, thirdly, in
polyphonic sentences, especially in the fugue, no individual voice
is heard to rise above lesser voices, but each voice (omitting
exceptions) takes equal part in the whole.

It is apparent that in all these cases consideration equal to
that given to the so-called melody or principal voice must be

bestowed on all the parts. Every part belongs to the whole; in each one the spirit of the poet lives and breathes. Let this above all be emphasized: there must be no haste in study, in forming the conception, so that parts which either are or appear to be important are alone considered, and seemingly unimportant ones are neglected. We must always remember that with Beethoven nothing is unimportant. It may be that one may have more importance than another, but even the subordinate belongs to the whole; the spirit has lived in it also, and has intended it to form a part of the whole. The seemingly insignificant accompaniment from the Finale of the small F-minor Sonata (page 46) has proved itself to be very important.

The repeated tones (quarter notes) in the bass of the D-major Sonata, Op. 28,

arc not mechanical percussions; they contain life; they press forward, and recede. In them, too, the spirit of the poet lives, and it has not been understood, if not recognized and made to be felt in the twenty-four measures of this one tone. The true Beethoven player puts his soul into every tone; for Beethoven himself has done the same.

After having recognized the contents and the significance of each voice in contrast to the others, all technical means must be directed toward making each one for itself recognizable, and toward carrying it out according to its character. This may not be neglected even where the separation seems apparently arbitrary. Beethoven often demands that a tone be sustained in one voice, while the same tone in another voice serves as a beginning to a figure or melody,—as in this measure (A)

of the G-major Sonata, Op. 31. The left hand has three voices to provide for: first of all, the large *G*, which the little finger must sustain throughout; secondly, the small *g*, which is each time to be held the length of a quarter; thirdly, between both sustained tones, the figure which at B is once more printed separately and which comes from the small *g*.*

To the ordinary player, notes with double stems mean only "theoretic circumlocution" or pedantry, while the true musician not only sees in them the signal of the coming together of two voices, but he will strive to bring this fact to the ears of his listeners. This small *g* which Beethoven so carefully supplies with two stems must be played more emphatically (*sf.*) and must be held longer; and the following tones of the figure must follow softly. The deep *G* must also be held firmly, and, so far as the instrument allows, must have a continuous tone, in order that it may form a quiet foundation. This will prevent the movable figure from becoming fundamental, and from destroying the quiet of the close which is here formed.

Now and then it seems advisable almost imperceptibly to separate the voices which are closely bound together, or to shorten one of them a trifle, in order that the more important voice may stand out. This might take place in the C-minor passage of the same Adagio the melody of which (A) becomes duplicated in the octaves.

---

* Taking for granted the sustaining of the thumb and little finger upon *g* and *G*, the fingering given at B is unavoidable; however, the sliding off of the second finger from *e-flat* to *d* is simple.

This doubling of the melodic tones is in accordance with the
great thought of the melody, but the entire passage is to be
played softly and delicately; and after six measures this fundamental temperament again unmistakably appears. Here the suggestion given at B (a frequent application of this would seem
weak and careless) might be applicable, but only for two measures. By this means the upper voice stands out. At C the octaves must be heard above the middle tone; they must be played
more strongly, and the middle tone may be shortened a very little ($\frac{1}{8}$ or $\frac{1}{16}$).

Again, in other places the contrast of the staccato and legato
effects will be helpful. Where the thought has once been recognized, the means will easily be found.

TEMPO AND METER.

THE observations heretofore have been confined to general laws and annotations, or have departed only imperceptibly therefrom. However, where can unbreakable and closely fitting laws be found in the realm of free spirit, the pulsations of sentiment, and the unrestrained fluctuations of fantasy? Whoever wishes to live and work in this realm must penetrate beyond all dictations, and in case of necessity, even go against them, in order to press forward to the one and only immutable law of reason,—all this, to respond to the demands of the idea, the being, as it were, of the contents.

One phase of this is now to be shown in tempo and meter, especially in Beethoven's works.

I. TEMPO.

The tempo (time) is, as is well known, the most general expression for the rate of movement of a tone series, and therefore of the life in which the same is to stand forth and operate. It is essential, therefore, to discover first the proper tempo, and then to follow it. The accomplishment of this is brought about by musical training in general. Establishment of tempo seems rather simple; for the composers themselves, at least the later ones—among them Beethoven—indicate the tempo. If only these indications were plain and always feasible! But this is by no means always the case. With reference to the old markings —Allegro, Adagio, etc.— this uncertainty has been recognized for half a century. It is well known that the Allegro movement is to be more rapid than the Adagio. But what is the absolute measurement of these movements? and are passages marked with the same tempo really all of the same rapidity of movement?

These doubts were, as is known, to have been removed by the Mälzel metronome,* by means of which, absolute measurement of movement can be given. Beethoven declared himself in favor of the metronome, and has marked several compositions metro-

---

*A pendulum arrangement which, according to its position, makes determined numbers of pulses in a minute.

nomically; for example, the Symphonies and partially the Quartets, up to Op. 95, inclusive; among the pianoforte works, only the large Sonata, Op. 106.* In the ninth symphony, however, it occurred that the master unconsciously gave two decidedly opposite metronomic indications, and finally declared, " No metronome at all! Those who have a right feeling do not need it, and those who have not, will not be helped by it." It is evident, therefore, that Beethoven did not overestimate the value of the metronome. However valuable the instrument may be to the composer, for a safe placing of the tempo desired by him, an absolute determination of the tempo is not in accordance with the spirit of art. The tempo is determined not only by the thought out of which a work of art has sprung, and by the manifold contents thereof, but also by the temporary mood of the performer; the amount of vibrating material (whether an orchestra is abundant or limited in numbers), the breadth of the room in which the tone waves are to be developed, require consideration. This probably explains (at least in part) the unanimous declaration of Czerny, Madame von Ertmann, and others who associated constantly with Beethoven, that he played his compositions differently every time.

We must therefore return to the old markings, which give at least approximate determinations, and which yield artistically favorable liberty both to the subjective feeling and to the demands of the moment, besides having authoritative value. It is true that even the old tempo marks have changed their measurements. The tempo is now taken much more rapidly. Mozart, complaining over the distortion of his compositions through exaggeration of the tempo, said: "Then you think it is here to be made fiery; well, if the fire is not within the composition, it will certainly not be brought into it through chasing." This truth, strong as it is, could not ward off the haste of vanity and inner voidness which is so easily attained. Finally, it must be conceded that the argument in regard to tempo can never come to a close, because it is dependent upon subjectiveness, momentary mental conditions, etc. (page 14). A general principle, however, remains: namely, the deeper and richer the content, the less does it allow haste; just as for an address of a speaker who desires to press on to an important end it is not fitting to use the tone of light, girlish talk; each has its quality and its place.

---

* It is well known that Beethoven's works were variously marked metronomically by later editors (Czerny and Moscheles). Such indications can of course only be considered as individual opinions of the editors, and ought therefore not to be accepted without test.

It is interesting to observe that in Beethoven himself a change took place in regard to this point. In his virtuoso period, when he still played his concertos himself, Reichardt, in 1808, heard him play his G-major Concerto, of which he says: "It is remarkably difficult, and performed by Beethoven with astonishing skill in the most rapid tempo." On the other hand, we find in the conversation journals of the spring of 1824 most important statements of Schindler. He says to the master, after the rehearsal for the concert ("Akademie") which took place May 7, 1824: "I wanted to embrace you yesterday, after the rehearsal, when you gave us all the reasons why you feel your works differently than you did fifteen or twenty years ago.* . . . . I confess openly, that I was in former years not always satisfied with this or that tempo, because I felt the meaning of the music differently. It was also plainly seen, and astonishing to many at the rehearsals in Vienna, that you wanted to have all the Allegros slower than formerly. I impressed the reason for this upon my mind— a remarkable difference! How much more now stands out in the middle voices, which before was entirely inaudible and often confused!"

The change in the choice of tempo may explain why even the degrees of velocity given by Beethoven may not be accepted without careful test. The old marking does not, at any rate, give an absolute tempo. Thus it appears that the first movement of the large F-minor Sonata, marked *Allegro assai*, simple as is its form, should not be taken too rapidly, on account of the depth of the contents, which demand the utmost expression. If the Finale marked Presto, of the F-major Sonata, Op. 10, were executed too rapidly, the humor of the passage would be lost. In matters of free fancy, the free spirit alone, and not the letter, can decide.

Whoever, taking for granted all the other demands, wishes to come to a certain conclusion as to the tempo, must not rashly yield to the impression of the first sentence; he must consult with the other passages, which from their inner being form therewith a relative whole. One might say he must consider the whole in order to decide on the whole; however, it is of advantage to bring forward important moments.

Now every large episode ("Satz") (going beyond the song form) contains two or more principal subjects (moments), called principal and secondary theme, or principal, secondary, and closing theme. Every part here mentioned may contain within itself

*One must imagine Beethoven's answer in the interval.

more than one theme.   All these themes are the principal moments of the composition, and at the same time the ruling ones
as regards the determining of the tempo, which must be in accordance with all these moments, not merely with one.   Now
for a few examples:

The first movement of the D-major Sonata, Op. 10, is marked
Presto, and justly so.   But what can we judge from that?   Beyond Allegro there are many degrees of velocity.   Judging from
the first theme,

the movement might be taken very rapidly; but soon after follows a second theme of the principal subject, in B minor,

which appears more meditative, less violent than the first.   The
same is true of the secondary theme of the "working out" of the
first motive ($\bar{d}$, | c-sharp, b, a), of the majestic climax of the same,
and the second closing theme.   Here it is well not to be too
hurried in the tempo.   The same advice might be given regarding
the first theme of the E-minor Sonata, Op. 90; here the complex-
ity and finesse of the rhythmic structure urge moderation.

Let us now consider the first movement of the large F-minor
Sonata.   The annotation, as before stated, is Allegro assai, and
might lead to exaggeration; the principal theme (page 49)
might lead hasty natures to a flying speed, although the admon-
ishing theme—d-flat, d-flat, d-flat, c—gives warning for deliber-
ation.   Now let us consider the martial song of the side theme:

Shall this too flit by?   Shall the rebellious percussions of the
sixteenth passage signify no more than an arpeggio étude?

Finally, let us examine the finale of the A-major Sonata, Op.

101. Beethoven has marked it Allegro, but has superscribed, in
addition, "quickly, but not too much so, and with decision."
For an accomplished player it is not impossible to play this
passage as fast again as is meet; but can the listeners be able to
perceive and feel all the voices which form the polyphonic network? It remains, therefore, a necessity to confer with the
whole in order to choose the tempo rightly. Such performers as
are inclined, either through impetuosity or delight in remarkable
representations, or urged on by pride (in showing themselves
eminent players), to exaggerate the tempo have here particular
assistance. For such players a rehearsal of the contents and
character of the composition is useless; they are not willing to
sacrifice their idiosyncrasy; they act unconsciously.

With such players we must deal according to their own personal interest. "If you really," we must ask them, "play the
Finales of the Sonatas,—Op. 26, 27², 53, 57,—twice as fast as
they ought to be played, do the sentences really become more
brilliant? Do they really grant you an opportunity of showing
yourselves as bravura players? Compare them with études and
concertos, which are really intended for display and bravura,
and you will at once perceive the difference; you will recognize
that these passages (and many others) aim at other ends, which
may be depreciated and fallen short of, but which one can never
transform. You spoil the work, without thereby attaining your
purpose."

2. METER.

The fundamental principle of measure is well known; so long
as the time is not expressly changed, all parts of the measure
have equal length. The application of this principle to the
pulses is the fundamental law. It is one of the first duties of the
teacher to develop in the pupil a perfect idea of rhythm, and
upon the perception thereof the quality of the performance depends. Indeed, a neglect of this threatens destruction to interpretation, and finally to the musical thought of the player. An
unrhythmic player is a bad pianist.

True as all this is, nevertheless, as is well known, multitudinous departures from this metric steadiness are often required.
In the works of all the composers we even find such deviations
annotated (through accelerando, ritardando, etc.), or expressed
in the contents of the composition. In no other composer are
these departures demanded more often than in Beethoven; with
him one must perceive metric freedom in addition to metric

repose, and must learn the appreciation thereof in order to do justice to his train of thought. Here, again, is a determining motive for the admission of pupils to the works of Beethoven,— at least to those which demand metric freedom. One who has not gained a perfectly uniform sense of rhythm cannot be admitted to the freedom of rhythmic variation without danger.

What signification, then, have these two extremes,— rhythmic repose and rhythmic freedom? This must be determined in order that both may be recognized beside each other, and that each may be made felt in its place.

Metric uniformity, evenness of movement, may in individual moments be the expression of the inner equiponderance of the tranquillity of the mind. However, this quietude cannot be considered a normal condition in the musically inspired and excited soul; it cannot exist in the plurality of musical moments. To these episodes, in which evenness acts according to inner laws, others are added for which some external law demands precision of movement. This is the case in marches and dances, where the precision of the march or dance movement determines the character of the meter. It may also be more or less the case with works whose contents and purpose remain remote from deeper emotion; such are Beethoven's Sonatas, Op. 22, 54, 53, the Finale of the Sonata, Op 26, and many passages more or less.

Rhythmic freedom — that is, the liberation from precision of movement — is the opposite of even, measured effect, and is therefore the expression of the liberated soul awakened to a more active life. Such life cannot be ruled by uniformity, for the movement must follow the order and power of the incentive. The manifestation in tone and word and gesture must respond to the pressing forward and the hesitating sentiment, if it is to be true. In fact, the nature of music throughout is that of speech. Metric variation, then, is a means of expression for the higher moments of life, natural truth and natural law. It is also the original form of utterance; for music existed a few thousand years before the structure of metric life was built.

Rhythmic firmness then came into use, as the highest but not always a justified demand of reason, in order to moderate the emotions which, alone, would be without boundary and without rest. Thus the ever-moving, wavering, and internally undecided and undetermined tone language secures a hold through the precision of rhythmic motion.

From this point of view, both opposites—freedom and lawfulness—achieve their deserved right. Let us adhere to the latter, because, and in so far as, it is directed by the composer. But let us be courageous and dutiful enough to depart from this, to freer measurements, where we are convinced that through this, and in no other way, the real intention of the composer can be expressed. That he has not always given particular directions—in fact, has done so comparatively seldom—ought not to be an obstacle to us; for we know how impossible it is for a composer to represent his conceptions, even approximately, were he to paint his paper black.

Here, again, it is essential to recognize the intention of the composer, to penetrate through the work—and beyond it, into his spirit. What position did Beethoven himself take in regard to this? The earliest witness is Ries, who from 1801 to 1805, from the age of fifteen to twenty, was Beethoven's piano pupil. He says of Beethoven: "In general he himself played his compositions very capriciously; however, he generally remained fairly within the bounds of even measure, and only occasionally hastened the tempo. Now and then he held back the tempo in his crescendo and ritardando, which gave a very beautiful and striking effect." Here unyielding rhythm appears as the overruling element. "At times" his tempo was said to have been hastened; "at times" to have been delayed, and "with most striking effect."

Schindler expresses himself differently. He says: "Whatever I have heard Beethoven play, was free from all restraint in time,—a tempo rubato * in the true sense of the word,—as contents and situation demanded, without, however, having the slightest inclination toward a caricature." Here freedom of movement is designated as the overruling element in Beethoven's playing; at the same time the suspicion of exaggeration and abuse (caricature) is warded off.

Both informations accord, inasmuch as both of them testify to the application of rhythmic freedom,—only that by Ries this is stated as exceptional, but by Schindler as the overruling manner of playing. How shall this departure be explained?

Ries heard Beethoven up to 1805, when he had not yet writ-

---

* The tempo rubato was a fashion of the eighteenth century, dating from the last half, and came from the singers of Italy and France. It was intended to replace the free, deep feeling which was wanting in the compositions themselves; this tempo rubato was therefore an untruth, and was soon compelled to yield to the reaction of reason. With this fashion (which amid other things became visible in Pergolese's Stabat Mater) Beethoven had nothing in common; he followed entirely the inner impetus—the demand of the thing—when he resorted to free movement.

ten his most important and spiritually freest works. At that time
Beethoven's thought itself was not yet developed to fullest freedom, as is shown by the uninterrupted and incalculably rising
progress of his works. Presupposably, Beethoven, especially in
his lesson hours, must have considered the position of his pupils,
and did not allow himself to play freely, in order not to give a
misleading example. Finally, Ries himself never attained that
high artistic development which would have required freedom
of expression, or at least would have been conducive to the
same. This is proved by his otherwise valuable works, and ren-
derings at the piano, also his opinions of the Eroica, the Over-
ture to the Ruins of Athens, etc. As an entirely different personality, with overruling mental development, Schindler several
years later came to Beethoven, and as friend and pupil remained
with him to the end. He could therefore observe the advanced
master from every side. "His older friends,"—so writes Schindler,—" who have followed the development of his spirit from
every direction, assert that he only took up this manner of playing in the third period of his life (beginning with 1813), and
that he had entirely departed from the former less expressive
manner."

Here, then, are two testimonies—a restrictive one, and a far-
reaching one—in order to convince us of a conviction which
requires no further proof, so securely is it rooted in the nature of
the case.* Besides, we also have, still further, a few authentic
revelations from Beethoven himself. In the autograph copy of
the song "Nord oder Süd," in Artaria's possession, there is distinctly written in Beethoven's hand, " 100 according to Mälzel;
but this can refer to the first measures only, for sentiment has
also its peculiar rhythm; but this cannot be entirely expressed
in this grade" (namely, 100). That in the very face of a prescribed degree of velocity, feeling may have an individual right,
"its own rhythmic progress," is not scientific, but has been expressed very plainly and beautifully by the master. Enough (if
not too much) has been said about the right of free rhythm, the
departure from evenness of movement in order to give to sentiment the means of expression in such moments when it has wan-
dered out of the equilibrium of its movement.

Metric variance, or departure from the fundamental pulse
measurement, can manifest itself in but two ways: in accelerating

* The author had come to this conviction long before the appearance of Schindler's work,
and had manifested the same with word, script, and deed. He rejoices, therefore, over his
agreement with this worthy man who enjoyed the distinction of being Beethoven's pupil and
friend.

or retarding the time. Either of these modes may take place in greater or lesser degree, can rule for a longer or shorter time, and both can change places with each other. The essential thing is contained in the two conceptions,—accelerating and retarding. But where does hastening and delaying, where the interchanging of parts, take place?

An accelerando is naturally essential where the mental poise steps beyond the original measurement. Such a case is existent in the Adagio of the C-sharp minor Sonata. The melody moves quietly and with dignity; it persists throughout in an even soul movement, therefore in equal pulse progression. Naturally the accompanying triplets of eighths must be carried out in perfectly even movement. But now the melody closes at the 28th measure. The following four measures may be considered supplementary; at any rate, from measure 32 the triplet movement (and this in prolonged duration) forms the only content. Not until measure 37 does the melodic motive of the supplementary phrase make itself known, and in measure 42 the melody returns again. The portion from measure 32 to measure 37 lacks the support of a definite melody; it desires it and strives after it, until it approaches the same in measure 37, and seizes it in measure 42. Lack of support, and desire, determine here a more intense movement, which, however, is far from becoming passionate; it may be but the expression of a restlessness soon to be overcome. It therefore rises only a little beyond the fundamental tempo of the passage, and having risen almost imperceptibly, returns shortly into its old tempo. Like moments might be found in the first movement of the D-major Sonata, Op. 10, or the Scherzo (asking pardon for the form name) of the other Phantasie Sonata, after the Trio, where the quarter notes are dissolved into eighths.

A retarding takes place where the intensity and excitement which has given the tempo to one passage diminishes. This requires no special explanation; a single illustration will suffice, and this is furnished in the first sentence of the Sonata "Les Adieux" (Op. 81). Toward the end of the first movement, the calls of those who are about to part, in the following passage.

and in this one at A—

and finally in their continuation at B (especially from A on for nineteen or twenty-one measures), appear to be repeated more and more distantly, and gradually to die away. A decrease of intensity (decrescendo) can only begin to take place at measure 13 with its full effect, which is to vanish into a mere echo. The determining means of expression is the gradually delayed move- ment. The following figure of eighths, however, strives after the original tempo; but this cannot be entirely restored.

Hurrying and delaying often become necessary in order to lead back from an opposite moment to the original time, and so that the return may not become a sudden plunge. For this reason it seems advisable to gradually give up the above-indi- cated holding back, as early as measure 19. So also in the pas- sage cited from the C-sharp minor Sonata, the return of the sequel (measure 37) might be used to lead back from the hurried move- ment into the original time.

Especially worthy of mention is the application of tarrying or delaying as an expression of meditation or emphasis, for the realization of which increased intensity does not suffice and is not adequate in itself. This may be observed in the first sen- tence of the D-major Sonata, Op. 10:

It is staccato and not legato; is marked piano at the beginning, and has under the last note the sign *sforzato*. But this last note is only the last point of the upward-striving sentence; it is not to be struck with an accent, but the whole sentence is to be increased. To attain this with increased intensity only, would lead to a coarseness of touch; the tones (*e, f-sharp, g, a̅*) must be gradually held back. Immediately after, the passage repeats itself and rises again from *a* to *a-sharp, b, c-sharp, d, e, f̅-sharp.* Upon these high tones, of which each one is marked *ff,* great power would not be attainable; they must be (*d, e, f-sharp*) remarkably held back.

If here the retard at the end of the sentence seemed applicable, the same can be done as well at the beginning or the middle. This is perceived in the triplet progression of the C-sharp minor Adagio which has been mentioned on a previous page. The tempo beginning with measure 3 must be intensified, and the figure would be greatly improved if there were a little retard upon the first triplet of every measure,—or in other words, in the progression of the first tone to the second,—and lastly, at the climax of the triplet figure.

(*Gis*)

The annotation ⌐ is only an incomplete indication. In all these and like cases, one can observe what is hinted on page 76; i. e., how an increase of velocity supports or takes the place of the intensity of power, when this does not suffice or is inapplicable.

But how—beside this metric freedom—is the pulse feeling and the fundamental evenness of time preserved, and how, therefore, the demand of the musician for firmness, gratified? for this is (page 71) a required thing; as important as an even balance to one who is running or walking, and as necessary as a return of quiet to the mind.

First, even balance should never be yielded up without good reason, and freedom should never be carried into exaggeration.

Second, though we may depart, with full right, in certain moments, from the even or original time, we must know how to return to this tempo. The original time may be compared to a straight line, the free movement to the waved line, which twines about the former like the life-signifying snakes around the firm staff of Mercury. Only very exceptionally the original time is lastingly given up; and when it is done, there are generally particular directions.

Finally, the poetic player finds still weighty means of keeping awake the metric feeling, even in passages where he frees himself from pulse regularity; and this is done by means of rhythmic accent. He designates (as has been shown at page 57) not only the metric construction through intensifying the important pulses of the measure, but he brings out also the higher significance of the passage, through gathering together and rounding off the parts, which stand in the same relation to measure construction as a verse, as a whole, to the single feet.

. Order and comprehension depend more upon these accents — which designate the construction of the whole, and which encompass themselves and melt together in the contents—than upon the holding fast to this entirely external evenness of tempo, which only knows how to create order by giving to like metric parts a strict tempo, entirely indifferent to the contents. Thus in accentuation is manifested the artistic, in the time keeping, the mechanical or abstractly intelligent spirit. Beethoven inclined so strongly to the former idea, that however much he loved and sought dancing, yet, according to the testimony of Ries, he never succeeded in dancing strictly in time. Schindler, on the contrary, testified that he emphasized the rhythmic accent with preference, and that he made frequent use of the "caesura and rhetorical pause." The former serves (as has been remarked, page 60) as the close of a section, the latter as a close to larger parts,—or also through a rhythmically entirely unassigned stop,—in order to call attention to the entrance of an important movement.

Strangely, such a rhetorical pause has even been written out, and we find it in the C-minor Symphony. The first sentence begins thus:

with a motive of two measures,—*g, g, g,* | *e-flat,*—of which the last tone is prolonged by a hold. This motive is repeated with *f, f, f, | d.* However, the last tone is twice as long; thus the motive is extended through three measures, and not until the third measure does the hold appear, which before appeared on the second. Beethoven has written a pause for this tarrying which is out of proportion with the length of the tones. Only then does the real Allegro passage begin; and to the master himself, the first five measures served only as introduction. Hereby he departs authentically from even measurement into metric freedom.

FORM OF STUDY.

NOW for a few words concerning the manner in which one can most successfully live into a work and make it one's own. Many considerations here make their demands. Spiritual understanding and technical control, the objective content of the work, and the subjective mood and direction of the performer,— each of these opposites has its undeniable right. Every claim must be made valid, yet it must not be allowed to destroy that of the others. It is particularly essential that the individuality of the performer be neither disturbed nor mutilated. He cannot work for himself, left to himself, but must accommodate himself to the idea of the composer, to the content of the work. If this subordination is forced, if perchance the teacher presses his own subjectiveness between that of the student and that of the work, he destroys self-determination, freedom, and *naïveté*,—one's own near feeling to the subject,— and thus the study becomes a lifeless, mechanical performance, and artistic success is simply impossible. Art without freedom of expression is a nonentity.

We teachers of either word or pen, however high we may stand or may think we stand, must resign all authority. We must do this. not only because among our still awkward and stupid pupils perhaps another Beethoven may be hidden, as the first one was hidden among Pfeiffer's and Neefe's pupils, and because our names, too, like those of Pfeiffer and Neefe, may in the future be mentioned only for his sake, but also because even the most ordinary pupil must be granted his human and artistic claim of self-judgment and self-determination, without which the most gifted pupil cannot attain his full development. I, who for a lifetime have taught so much, have never desired to place authority over my pupils, but have constantly warned them of every authority,—particularly of that which they tried to attribute to me; and I have incessantly directed and led them according to the voice of their own feeling and thinking. Only in this way can we secure genuine men and artists. The way seems longer and more laborious in the beginning, but it soon proves itself to be the shortest, and that which alone leads cheerfully to the end.

When the study of a particular work is undertaken, he who wishes to acquire it ought first to play all the movements, in their proper order, entirely through one or more times, allowing no interruption or hindrance,—not even through consciousness of errors in playing,—and without accepting advice from elsewhere, either preparatory to or assisting in the work. This first playing must be done at once in the tempo which seems to the player to be the correct one, whether or not his technical skill be equal to the difficulties of this tempo. A temporary tarrying in the movement on account of these difficulties is inadmissible. Hereby acquaintance with the work is begun undisturbedly, and in absolutely naïve manner, as a result of which the student has secured a more or less correct and complete approximate representation of its direction and content. This first cursory attack of the work must then be followed by the real and more accurate study, which has two directions,—study directed to the content of the work, and that which is directed toward the technical. Both ends should be pursued side by side; not at the same time, from moment to moment, but one to follow the other. If here in this book the technical is placed first, it is only because this can be disposed of more rapidly.

At the first playing, the first glancing through, the player must have been impressed with those passages which manifested technical difficulties, causing misconstructions, possibly, at the first playing. These misconstructions—by which we mean errors which arise only from momentary inattention—must be observed and avoided. At the first glance an entire part may often seem difficult, while upon closer investigation only a portion—frequently only a very small portion—is the real seat of the difficulty. Furthermore, a part, a passage may appear, step for step full of newness and difficulty, while later, a single small motive (or a few motives) shows itself as the root of the whole, through the mastery of which the entire passage is conquered. Here, again, insight into the structure of a work of art serves to conquer the same.

If such a technical difficulty has been found, it is necessary to investigate whether the passage does or does not return in the course of the composition; for as a rule, every sentence and every passage of a composition is applied two or more times, and is conquered in the same or like manner. Thus every passage which requires practice, inclusive of its repetitions, becomes the object of special technical study. This is more methodical and helpful than when the internally varied demands are mixed together, whereby the second takes away from the first, and the power of all is scattered over many demands, instead of being directed to one end at a time.

By the side of this technical practice the artistic study of the work goes on. Even the first performances must have made at least a general impression, and must have called forth a judgment, though it may have been very general and uncertain in the beginning. This impression should be kept in mind by a characteristic word, without at first exerting oneself hypercritically, or yielding up to it as though it were a law which could not be broken. Only gradually do we penetrate into the truth and into its fundamental origin,—some of us more rapidly, others more slowly, and perhaps, on that account, more surely and deeply. To me, the writer of this book, the content of the Sonata Op. 109, after an acquaintance of thirty years, just began to be plain when I wrote the "Beethoven"; and many things in the last Quartets did not appear to me until I wrote the second edition of that work. I do not ask if others arrived at this point more rapidly, or found more in it,—for indeed, how many have lived into the second part of "Faust," or into the truth of the Passion according to Matthew, who have been acquainted with these subjects thirty years?

As judgment begins to dawn, the larger portions of the work will appear in their correct light, and the student begins to discriminate characteristically; and though the first glimpses may be uncertain, they will soon reveal light. Take, for example, the E-minor Sonata, Op. 90, with its two movements: how the second, in its melting tenderness, stands out against the first energetic one! Can there still be an internal unity between them? Again, take the A-flat major Sonata, Op. 26, which begins with its contemplative variations and eventually introduces the Funeral March upon the Death of a Hero. Both movements may be obvious at first; much less certain, however, the (so-called) Scherzo just before the March; and how is the Finale to be interpreted? Similarly, one might soon hope to find oneself at home in the C-sharp minor Sonata, Op. 27, in the Adagio and Finale; but how about the middle movement, the Allegretto? Many a capable player has demonstrated that he has not understood it; indeed, the noble Louis Berger once suggested that it be left off entirely.

However great or inadequate the impression of these first glimpses may have been, we have thereby stepped across the threshold of the tone structure, have in the spirit looked into the great halls, have noticed their differences, have drawn into consideration their relationship, or the apparent absence of relationship; and we are therefore ready to take up the study of individual parts or passages. In these, again, we find members and parts which serve as end and support to investigation. . They are the various parts or themes of which we find two or more in every large composition. Whoever understands composition — or at least has obtained an insight into form — will without difficulty recognize the larger parts of the whole,— principal theme, counter theme, closing theme, parts first, second, and third,— and will thereupon recognize and be able to gain a deeper insight into the content. But without this knowledge the more attentive searcher might penetrate readily into this tone structure.

Let us take, for example, the first movement of the Pathétique Sonata. The very first glance reveals two different parts,—the introduction, marked Grave, and the first part of the Allegro. This is followed by a reminiscence of the introduction, which is then followed by the second part (according to general, everyday expression; but according to the language of art we would need to say the second and third part) of the Allegro. Where the close is expected, a suggestion of the Grave again appears, and a passage of the Allegro closes. This entire observation is, so to speak, self-evident, for these passages are marked by closing bars and annotations, so as to be comprehensible to even an entirely inexperienced eye. The passages Grave and Allegro differ according to tempo and content; they are opposites, but they form an inseparable whole (neither closes itself), and must therefore bear an internal relationship to each other. How can the character of each be discerned, and how can their relationship be made manifest? In the Allegro, the first theme (Hauptsatz) becomes visible at once to the connoisseur of form. Although he may not be entirely certain of the content, beginning with measure 16 or 17, the broad close at B-flat and the passage

in E-flat minor will certainly reveal itself by the new content, and especially by the dialogical form (bass and soprano alternate in the melody). He may possibly, in amateur fashion, call it

second theme; but it is in reality the side theme (Seitensatz).
Just as clearly must the following E-flat passage appear to him
as a new theme, and whether or not he may find therein a closing
theme, or whether he may know of the necessity of such at all,
he certainly will perceive the tendency to a close as felt in the
E-flat major part. A repetition of the first theme, carried into
E-flat major, closes the first part.

Hereby the content of the entire Allegro is fully shown as
to its inner being; and whoever has recognized the three parts
will again find in part second (and third) that figure which, beginning with measure 25, formed itself out of the first sentence.
This continues until, after a broad close on G, the principal subject again appears in C minor, and then the third part begins.
The entire content of the first part appears again, then the
Grave, and lastly, again the principal subject of the Allegro.
Casually, the structure of the first movement of the D-minor Sonata, Op. 31, might be compared with this.

Thus the content of the Pathétique Sonata (at least the first
movement) may have become somewhat clear. There are three
distinct parts, the first two of which are different, and yet related:

the second, however, is formed out of the first; the third is composed of two entirely different passages (the arpeggio and the
diatonic). There are, therefore, in all, five noticeable and significantly manifest sentences. Each one of these returns two or
more times, and oftener in a new form. Between them we find
intermediate themes, significant but subordinate, because they
naturally cannot appear independently, serving themselves only.
Thus, for instance, the principal sentence from measure 1 to 9
appears firm and closed as to its key and rhythm, while the middle member, measure 17 to 21, has not attained either of these
qualities. How, then, is the first sentence to be understood? and
how the second, coming out of the first? How does the second
sentence appear in its transformations in the second part? How
can the character of each of these five sentences be perceived
and brought into varied functions and relationships? and what
change in the tone color of interpretation does the transformation of these sentences demand?

The second example is found in the first Allegro of the E-flat major Sonata, Op. 7, a movement which to the unfamiliar glance is by no means so transparent as the one cited before.

The Allegro starts out without introduction. The principal theme.

announces itself and its motive (A) plainly enough, and the latter remains recognizable even in its transformation (B). Less clear to an unfamiliar eye might be the following passage, until, after a long delay on the bass tone, F, a second sentence (C)

clearly presents itself, after the completion of which a third (D), then in the new key (C major) a fourth (E),

and again, in B-flat major, a fifth sentence (F) appears. Only the beginnings will be cited. The connoisseur of form would designate these four sentences as side themes. Still two more distinctly distinguishable sentences close the first part; they might be called the closing themes.

We have, then, before us, not counting the middle members, seven different sentences. What is the meaning of each? How may they be distinguished? How are they united into a perfect whole, and how do they work themselves out? The principal theme (Hauptsatz), or, rather, only its motive (A), opens the second part. It soon yields, however, to the motive of the closing theme (Schlussatz), and returns again, in order to form itself into a new sentence (the eighth). All these appear in foreign keys; at first the motive of the principal theme, eliminating the more extended part which has been attached to it, steps into C minor; the motive of the closing theme appears in F minor and G minor, while the former travels again into A minor and D minor. The close appears in D minor; but instead of the broad close which presented itself in the Pathétique Sonata, we find it unsteady, and the return to the principal key is through a single somewhat indefinite chord, which soon vanishes away. This completes the second part; and now the third begins, with its principal theme in E-flat major, after which the entire series of seven sentences of the first part appear in their original order. But the third of these (D) is not yet satisfied. This subject, the most persuasive of all, appears again, where the close was expected, as a sort of sequel, and in contemplative transformation, after which the closing theme returns, in order to bring about the final close. These eight sentences must be conceived of characteristically; in a few (for example, sentences 1 and 2, 2 and 3, 4 and 5) the differences are brought to the surface, while in others (for example, 3 and 4, the continuation of 1 and 2 and 5) we are impressed with the relationship. Of all these themes the first and third receive the most attention.

This much in order to show how the construction and relationship of these passages can be made intelligible, and how certain points may be gained which will lead into the conception of the entire content. Thus the feeling of the work, so full of content, which hastens by in ever-changing forms, will not soar along in uncertainty. A dissection such as has been suggested would, after a few playings over, take even an inexperienced student only a very few minutes; and the characterizing of parts should never be accomplished searchingly or laboriously; often a hastily seized word suffices, and perhaps the next moment brings a happier one.

Lastly, the final study appears,—namely, the working out of every sentence in detail, and combined therewith, the melting of all details into a single unit. By this means the player has conquered the work in so far as was possible to his individual subjectivity; and though he may have failed now and then, he has preserved an independence, a freedom of emotion and judgment, without which there is no life possible in art or in art culture. The time has then come when it is necessary to be advised by others,—either verbally or otherwise,—and to test these verdicts by one's own conception. Nor should these first conceptions be dropped at once, upon hearing the differing opinions of teachers and advisers; on the other hand, they should not be adhered to stubbornly or anxiously, for it is not what *I* wish, not what *you* will, but what Beethoven desired; and this must be sought out by one's individuality as well as by help of experienced advisers.

Every advice must be listened to and tested, and finally the decision falls back upon the spirit of the interpreter. The most superior of all advisers, as regards Beethoven, is always Beethoven himself, as is natural. We know also that he not only played his works with sentiment,—as regards tone, and by giving himself up to an indeterminate feeling, but that he often undertook to utter internally-related mental conditions; that he often allowed himself to be influenced and carried away by external in-influences; that he created life; that he constructed ideally, as a Goethe in words and a Raphael in forms. But granted that we might avail ourselves of all subjective impressions, we still could not imagine that we had conceived of a Goethe or a Raphael, unless we had penetrated through to the idea of their creations. The same is true of Beethoven. That he frequently took upon himself demands such as are indicated above (not always, but often) we have sufficient proof. He has frequently given the thought content of his tone structures in writing. The names of the Eroica, and the Pastoral symphony (here the designation of single movements according to their content) are well known; the Funeral March upon the Death of a Hero, in the A-flat major Sonata, the titles "Les adieux, l'absence, le retour" of the three movements of the Sonata, Op. 81, and other names or designations, testify to this. When a complete edition of his works was in process, Beethoven had the idea (so writes Schindler) of indicating the thought content wherever he had not yet done so. In single works (for example, the Sonata, Op. 101) the multitudinous and impressive annotations indicate that he was led on by special and powerful mental conditions and representations.

Besides his own revelations, the testimonies of pupils and friends come to the rescue. Ries had, as it were, lived through with the master the origin of the Finale of the F-minor Sonata. Schindler has communicated several facts worthy of mention, in regard to the leading representations of the Beethoven compositions. Added to these comes Czerny, with absolutely positive testimony, and he especially may appear truthful, for two reasons: first, because he devoted years of his life to interpreting

Beethoven's compositions, after having been taught them by the master himself, and was therefore an ear-witness of the statements of the master; secondly, because, during a life of untiring and endless activity for development of technique, he proved himself to be one in whom fantasy, idealism, spirit of art, had not become the ruling motives, so that he would not have been able to introduce into the works or words of the master fantasies of his own. Even though he might have done so unconsciously, he could not of himself conceive of the ideal life which Beethoven lived, and which was so foreign to himself.

Czerny* states very positively: "It is true that Beethoven became inspired to many of his most beautiful works through his reading matter, or out of the visions brought out of his own native fantasy, and that we could only reach the true key to his compositions and their interpretation, through the certain knowledge of the circumstances — if this were everywhere possible." Czerny adds that "he was not communicative on this subject,— only occasionally, in confidential moods," which statement is confirmed by that of Schindler, who asserts that Beethoven did not seem to delight especially in determined or detailed verbal interpretations of others; and this might easily be perceived. Indeed, a certain spiritual modesty would prevent the artist from dissecting, as it were, his picture with words; for just as the poet could not fully substitute the painter, or the musician the poet and painter, so he above all others must feel that no words can fully interpret and exhaust his tone picture; that they can only indicate the content.

Again, Czerny says of the Adagio of the C-major Sonata, Op. 2: "In this Adagio the dramatic direction is developed, through which Beethoven later created a form of composition in which instrumental music became the expression also of painting and poesy. It is not only the expression of feeling that one hears; but one sees pictures and hears the stories of events."

Thus far Czerny's statement is powerful, for he had opportunity of listening to Beethoven's communications, which were to guide the interpretation, and he thus observed how the master was often guided by determined representations. Whether, on the other hand, Czerny's statements in regard to single parts are as reliable, remains to be tested in every case; for here misconceptions and many other things may have passed along with the rest. Even in the above-named Adagio, Czerny's statement in

---

* " Piano School," part 4, chapter 2, page 62.

regard to the same cannot be considered as being well founded, when he asserts, in regard to the Finale of the large F-minor Sonata: "Beethoven (who with such delight painted scenes from nature) may perhaps have thought of the singing of the sea on a stormy night, while from the distance comes a cry for help; at any rate, such a picture may convey to the player a suitable idea to the interpretation of this large tone picture." The very historic origin of the passage stands opposed to its interpretation as a storm at sea. Elsewhere Czerny states, in regard to the Finale of the D-minor Sonata, Op. 31: "The theme of this tone poem Beethoven improvised when he (1803) saw a rider gallop past his window. Many of his most beautiful works arose in this manner." Apart from the fact that this sonata was composed in 1802, it would be difficult to discover in this internally agitated but externally calm, tenderly formed tone figure, the clattering stroke of the gallop and the hastening by of the rider. And even if this were possible, the contemplative picture of the tone poet would become clad in the beggar garment of trivial circumstance.

Czerny, then, as ear-witness, has asserted that Beethoven often followed determined representations in his works. Whether, however, he everywhere truly gave the Beethovenian instructions, or whether he may have misconceived and therefore misrepresented many things, remains to be investigated. Most true is his statement that without recognition of the leading and determining representations, one cannot arrive at a full comprehension of his compositions; and that this comprehension assists in founding the proper interpretation. How this takes place, how the spiritual understanding, the ideal foundation out of which the tone structure has grown, acts upon the interpretation, upon the play of the fingers,— that is the original point of investigation; namely, how thought and will act upon the executing spirit. More cannot be said of this. Let the interpreter become filled with the idea of the poet, let his soul become kindled thereby, then let it work out as it will.

There are, however, further means and methods of bringing the feeling—and with it the power of interpretation—nearer to the intentions of the tone poet, and of possessing oneself of the finest means which would be absolutely impossible for verbal instruction. The first is observation of the playing of soulful pianists. The benefits derived are so self-evident as to require no further explanation. The second is observation of violin playing of artists who have a delicate enough conception; such as Laube, Wieniawski, Joachim. The violin for expression of melody is far superior to the piano, in that it is able to sustain a tone for a long time, to unite two or more tones absolutely, and in that it allows one tone to melt into another; while the piano can only utter tones which soon die away, and which only have the appearance of melting together. Let the pupil listen to great violinists, let him become filled with the feeling and the living representation of their playing, then let him seek as far as possible to carry them over to the piano. A third means is offered to all who can sing,—for the voice also controls the potent means for a soulful representation of the melody; added to this, one feels more deeply in singing—with body and soul, as it were—than one does in playing or in listening to an instrument. Sing Beethoven's melodies and you will feel them more soulfully, and therefore play them so. Beethoven constantly sang while composing; most composers have done so, not from an external requirement for representing the tones, but from an unconscious impulse to perceive them more deeply.

A last means for perceiving Beethoven more comprehensively is given to those who have an idea of the sound of various instruments. Without doubt, Beethoven, who lived so deeply in the world of instruments after his fifteenth year, possibly unconsciously carried orchestral representations over to the piano. Whoever can decipher him in such passages, can use the results of his research for the expression at the piano. The very first work which we will investigate will serve as a sample.

THE INDIVIDUAL WORKS.

Prefatory Remarks.

IT is stated on page 18, that not all works will be considered here, nor will any of them be taken up entirely; for this would seem somewhat unnecessary and circumlocutional. Indeed, it might seem even detrimental, in that it would limit the scope of individual research on the part of the student. The disciple and friend of art should be inspired and guided to investigations of his own; never should such research be taken from him, by accomplishing results for him. He ought, then, to test those things which have been indicated in the individual works; and having convinced himself as to their correctness, he should apply them in other works which offer similar instances.

In view of this, the first works will be analyzed more in detail than the later ones, which, it is supposed, will have been impressed by what has been said of the preceding.

The analysis of every work here is planned with reference to what has been said in the biography,* because a repetition here seemed incongruous. There is, however, no absolute need for the reader to return to the biography, for the attempt has been made to give the most essential points in this work.

F-minor Sonata, Op. 2.†

A tenderly flowing—one might say feminine—spirit pervades this Sonata. Tenderness and elegiac sentiment is its fundamental idea, out of which, however, it rises to passionate excitement. In accordance with this, its form does not possess massiveness; it is light, restricted mostly to one voice (with simple accompaniment) or to two voices; a richer network of voices exists nowhere. Even the first, most cursory glance teaches that great intensity, a real fortissimo, is absolutely out of the question. Wherever such an annotation is given in the first sentence, it only implies an intensified sforzato. In the Finale it only indicates the highest intensity which is applicable to this Sonata, and which is of an entirely different texture from the fortissimo in other works. It is clear, then, that the greatest, or at least a very

---

* "Beethoven, Life and Works," third edition.
† Biography, Part I, page 100.

great, degree of intensity—in passages marked *ff*, for example—

Prestissimo.

is here absolutely impossible.

That which has been denied in this direction must be attained by nicest gradation of the admissible degree of intensity, by accentuation, and, by way of compensation for intensity (page 76), through accelerating and retarding the movement. Here again the most careful time measurement with reference to the character of the composition must be observed; metric freedom must be reduced to the smallest limits, and the transitions from accelerated and retarded tempos must only be felt, as it were,—not, however, be made noticeable.

The very first movement represents at once the fundamental character of the entire Sonata. Even the passionate excitement of the Finale does not withdraw from it this characteristic. The principal subject (Hauptsatz) lies mainly in the melody of the upper voice; the accompaniment is entirely subordinated. How the beginning of this melody is to be played has been shown.

The first two measures are the heart or motive thereof, while in the two following measures the same is repeated in a higher position, is therefore intensified. Here, however, the progress is impeded; the last tones of the principal sentence become deeper, then are carried again into a higher sphere, until finally the highest tone, c̄, is taken with increased power, and the close comes in hesitatingly (for no satisfactory close has been attained). The rendering of the passage might be expressed thus:

The rising and descending line* indicates increase and decrease of intensity; the movement hastens and delays in similar man-

*It ought to be a wave line.

ner,—however, in imperceptible gradations. The accents (')
serve especially to lift out single tones; a-flat, measure 2, b-flat,
measure 4, a-flat, measure 5, b-flat, measure 6, c, measure 7,
should be retarded a trifle,—more especially the c and the following eighths, which sink into almost an *andante* movement. The
same is true of the following quarters, and the appoggiaturas are
to be played tenderly and a little retarded. All this must take
place without hesitation; the metric feeling must be kept alive by
rhythmic intonation.

This venturesome undertaking of drawing on paper, as it
were, a melody, according to degrees of intensity and movement,
can only be feasible with the first melody which is here to be
considered. A like change in movement and intensity will be
found applicable in all melodies in which the wave-like progress
of feeling finds expression. The passage, differently turned, repeats itself, and the execution must be the same as before. The
close of the sentence falls upon measure 8 of the repetition, and
the following measures

serve but to strengthen the same, while the tones, *e-flat, d-flat, c,*
demand gentle emphasis and a slight retard, both of which qualities are increased a second time. This must speak out, as it were,
with special emphasis,—as for instance, a serious speaker would
say, "It is true; it is absolutely true!"

The tempo is reëstablished in the following measure (by
means of the figure of eighths in the bass). Here the side
theme (Seitensatz) appears; though closely related to the principal subject (Hauptsatz), it is opposite in character, and its aim
is to progress downward, as that of the preceding was to rise.
(This is spoken of on page 62.) The figure of eighths in which
this terminates, urges forward with power and movement, hesitates at the repetitions from *d, a-flat, d,* and *g, f-flat, g,*—for the
composer also hesitates to continue on his path; then a new
pressing forward follows, and lastly the soaring runs of eighths
in accelerated movement. At the repetition the first tones (*a-
flat, f, e-flat, d-flat*) would receive special emphasis, through gentle holding back and a different accentuation, and the scale

passage would receive new life, while the closing subject (Schlussatz) follows more deliberately and with stronger emphasis.

I speak of the run of eighths—it is really nothing but the simple scale through two or three octaves—as soaring; and indeed it must thus stand out amid the relationship of the whole, and the gradual raising of the temperament. Not the single moment decides over its significance, but the internal relationship of all, in their contrasting forms. Thus the painter cannot paint light,—that is, light itself; but he may delude us through the contrast of light and darkness.

Considerable seems to have been said here concerning this short movement, and yet it is by no means exhausted; and the watchword must be — *Soul in every tone.* Even the accompaniment of the principal subject demands attention; the four pulses

are increased up to the last, upon which the melody begins again.

This will suffice for the first part.

The second part repeats the principal subject and then the side theme. Thought and expression are naturally the same. The side theme buries itself in the bass; and this must be indicated by the first tones of each phrase (*a-flat, g, g-flat, f, f-flat, e-flat*), for in its continuation the sentence sinks until it loses itself, as it were, in syncopations.

The Finale, only, requires further special attention. It breathes storm and passion, but that of a tenderly constituted soul; nowhere do we find massive power or highest vibration of intensity (page 58) applicable, and only the tempo, *prestissimo,* and still more, the intensifying and calming of both movement and intensity, can, aside from the single intonations, lift the movement up to its true significance.

The tempo must be taken so rapidly that the triplets of eighths in the accompaniment—for example, at the beginning, and at the entrance of the side theme.

must melt, as it were, into an up-surging and down-falling vibrating mass. This produces a storm-like effect, especially in

the closing theme (page 46), where the accompaniment begins
pianissimo, swells without interruption for six measures smoothly
to a fortissimo, and again calms itself in the following two measures. This tempo is also applicable to passages in which the accompaniment (at the close of the first and third parts) becomes
significant of its own accord.

Nevertheless, the tempo cannot be held steadily throughout.
It remains steady in the first entry of the principal theme, in
which the refractory, angry strokes become intensified when
marked piano, as well as when forte,

and must be broken off abruptly. There must be a retard at the
second appearance of the principal theme, beginning with *A-flat*
(measure 5), only the close returns to the first tempo, which then
continues up to the closing subject.

After the shattered condition of the principal theme, after
the impetuous raging of the side theme,

which introduces every phrase violently, then lets it die away,
the soul requires support in order not to fly away, and the music
has of course a like desire; this brings forth the closing theme,
with its satiated and repeated melody. It appeals to us as does
the first fleeting and almost threatening thought of a frightened
soul to a helper and avenger above. Control is still wanting,
and all flies along amid the storm. This sentence must not lose
its tempo; but while the accompaniment holds fast to it, the
tones (quarter notes) of the melody allow themselves to be
dragged along against their will,—for it (the melody) seems to
desire to stay; so that in their hesitating obedience, a so-called
tempo rubato is formed (page 73).

That for which the closing theme has paved the way is accomplished in the second side theme (which follows the first
part); it is nothing less than the expression of greatest devotion,

of prayer, which alone by itself, even without fulfillment, becomes a benefaction of comfort and inner recovery. The movement must here be made more gentle (but inconspicuously), the
touch must be tender, the melody carried in wave lines and made
to speak through its emphasis. The player must not accomplish
this externally, not according to the dictates of reason, but he
must take the contents of the sentence into his soul.

In this second side theme we find what has been mentioned before,—the influence of orchestral representations upon
the composition. It is not necessary to find evidence for this, for
it is hardly supposable that Beethoven consciously carried in-
strumentation in mind. Nevertheless, anyone who is at all conversant with orchestral instruments will recognize the echo of
them on the piano, and will be able to take this recognition as a
model for his performance.

This second side theme (trio part) consists, in the first
part, of,—1. A song figure of ten measures; 2. Its repetition in
the higher octave, with a few changes at the beginning; 3. A
new theme; and 4. Its repetition, in somewhat changed form,—
four plus four measures; 5. The first theme in octaves and trans-
formed; 6, 7. Repetition of 3 and 4, also in varied form; and
lastly, 8. Repetition of 5.

Here begins the transition to the third part, with triplets of
eighths. This second side theme (1 to 8) is written most
simply, and absolutely full of feeling. At 1 there appears almost
irresistibly the idea of the clarinet, with its soulful, swelling
sound:

at 2 the thought is directed to the flute, which is so closely related to the former, but which is smaller and not so warm. The
piano also finds less vibration for 2 than for 1, and the transpo-
sition is well founded. It is worth while investigating whether
or not we hear the oboe at 3, at 4 the related but more elastic
violin, and at 5 the flute and clarinet (or, more ideally, flute and
bassoon). The player should, however, not attempt to imitate
the physical side of the instruments, but should endeavor to
express their character.

With the assistance of the triplets of eighths — two measures each — the tempo is led back; the intervening measures of two each, with progression of quarter notes, constantly retard the tempo a little, until the triplet figure, and with it the first tempo, asserts itself.

Even in this first Sonata the natural rhythmic freedom, which is so severely censured by many, asserts itself; and indeed, it cannot be otherwise. We must, however, remember the caution of proceeding carefully, making no unnecessary departures; not only to satisfy metric feeling during this departure, through intonation, but also to return at the right time to the original movement. Without this the performance loses dignity and energy, and finally makes a caricature of the composition.

A-major Sonata, Op. 2.*

This Sonata unfolds before our eyes a moody picture of ever-changing life. Every moment must be quickly perceived and boldly placed, for the next instant may bring something entirely new. Nevertheless, changed as are its features, the whole grows out of an internal unity; and this must be brought out in its performance.

The principal subject of the first Allegro announces itself lightly and shyly,

then boldly and progressively, in order to broaden out into the quarters, and to give place to a new passage, three-voiced and in fleeting eighths, which takes a more quiet movement in the last measures. After the closing chord (measure 20) the rest may be made a little longer, after which the first motives reappear, then the passage of eighths, which is introduced by the up-beat of a triplet of sixteenths. The first motives must remain in tempo, but the passage of eighths cannot assert its repose after them, for a run of triplets of sixteenths bursts in upon them, places itself as a contrast to the eighths, which eventually gain the upper hand after all, and which, together with the quarter notes in the melody and a sustained bass, form the close of the principal subject and also the transition to the counter-subject.

* Biography. Part I, page 105.

One seems to see an incurious youth, who does not know what to
do with his up-bubbling life. Whoever holds fast to this picture,
finds the representation of his own accord. A synopsis might be:
the beginning light and bold, the passage of eighths beginning
lightly, then flying through all the voices, with slight stress upon
the upper voice, measure 12 to 14 of the bass, then the run of
sixteenths violently dashing upward; there cannot possibly be
another way of rendering this.

After the impassioned and unsteady principal subject, the
side theme, marked "espressivo," appears, plaintively, one
might say regretfully, in E minor. The melody of three-times-
four measures starts more emphatically with the first three tones,
sinks together, as it were, each time, and therefore demands a
decrease of tempo and intensity. But the rolling figure of the
first principal subject tears it away from its humility, a new running passage (it is given on page 34 for technical reasons) again
restores the bold mood, and out of the well-known passage of
eighths the closing theme, sinking into gentle calmness, is developed.

The second part is occupied first with the first, then with the
second principal subject, both of which he carries to a broader,
more energetic development. This is especially true of the first,
which from its piecemeal beginning now melts into a firm whole.
The performer must here follow the thought of the composer,
and must raise his performance to a similar energy of touch and
expressiveness, until the passage itself sinks to rest. The passage of eighths again returns in its familiar manner, and at measures 19 and 20 seems to wish also to go to rest; but just at this
point it bursts forth with new energy.

Here the three voices appear, one after another; the second
continues in the tones *e, f,* which, on account of more ready execution, are written in the form of appoggiaturas to the first voice.
Each voice must be played in the same manner, with similar

energy; in each one the triplet of sixteenths must powerfully commence the next eighth. Further than this nothing need be said, as the following contents are familiar.

The Largo following is marked "appassionata,"—not (according to the sense of the word) to indicate passion, but only to point out the deep, thoughtful content which is heard therein. The song is quiet and majestic, like the meditation of a noble soul in loneliness under a starry sky. Whoever can become filled with this picture will succeed in understanding all the details, and therefore their reproduction.

The principal subject shows two different figures appearing simultaneously: first the melody of the upper voice, closely melting into the two middle voices; and secondly, the agile, forward-moving bass, which is to give out its tones very short until it arrives at the legato eighths. Its melody moves along quietly, generally step for step, the melody of the upper voice (*f-sharp, f-sharp, f-sharp,* | *e, f-sharp,* | *g, f-sharp,* | *c*) still more quietly, so that the progression of quarters (at measure 5) becomes significant. The whole must be quiet, yet by no means weak; the three upper voices must come together with absolute precision, so that the chords stand out gently but sonorously; at the same time the upper voice must be heard almost imperceptibly above the others, and the intonation of the more important moments

must result without the destruction of the gentleness of soul and tone movement, and equality of the middle voices; *g* in the third and *b* in the sixth measure must be heard as climaxes. The bass becomes emphatic through its movement and fuller tone combination, while in intensity it is similar to the middle voices, or at least must not conspicuously be heard over them.

In the little intermediate theme which takes the place of a second part, the tones *a, g-sharp, a,* in upper and lower voice (the latter of which takes it from the former), need to be heard more distinctly; they are the heart of the passage. The first part is remarkably intensified at its return (as third, or close of the second), and Beethoven has marked the climax of this intensification *ff.* The highest intensity, however, will come into use later; here we must increase to forte; and the last two intense tones—*f-sharp* and *e*-- of the melody must receive emphasis by a retarded movement. The greatest intensity appears only when, in the Coda, the theme in minor appears *ff* in the very beginning.* At this climax, which the bass accomplishes with its passage of forward-pressing eighths, the entire vibratory power must be applied, and must be made even more significant through a delaying of the first two eighths, in the first and second measures of the passage. It is a forcible moment, which towers most emphatically over the entire Sonata, and which stands beyond all doubt as to its demands and content.

A last remark in regard to the Minore of the Scherzo. In the beginning of the first part

the lower voice (*ē*, | *c̄*) is the really melodic one; the upper one with its *f̄, ē, d̄, c̄* enters only imitatively, and therefore it must take part only imitatively in the performance of the first. This is indicated above. The initial tones of both voices demand a slight emphasis; and all this can only be accomplished by a position of the hand (page 50) suited thereto. Naturally the same manner of playing is applied to the repetitions.

E-flat Major Sonata, Op. 7.†

This is one of the finest tone structures which we possess, the first sentence being a rich wreath of most manifold blossoms, and arranged in most complete harmony; for the whole has arisen from a single impulse in the spirit of the tone poet. It is therefore not sufficient if the interpreter comprehend rightly the individual moments only; he must be able to express the relationship of one to the other, and hence their unity. The first

---

*Is not this assumption, especially the remark of the first *ff*, in opposition to Beethoven's annotations? By no means. *ff* does not always mean "the very strongest"; but very strong,—stronger than forte. Like every intensity mark, and like the statements in regard to time, it comprises many gradations, which must be chosen each time according to the thought contained. Beethoven has marked *ff* for the close of the principal subject, for the close of the side theme (12 and 13 measures, further on), and directly after it *p*: again *f* for the principal subject in minor, which, however, requires considerable intensifying in itself, in the passage of eighths. Are these moments of the same value? Certainly not. Beethoven, or rather the language of art, was only devoid of sufficient marks for all gradations of forte.

† Biography, Part I, page 161.

part of the first movement of this Sonata has seven principal
moments, which are here pointed out as to their beginning,

and supplied with letters. A is the principal theme; C, D, E
are side themes; F, G, and H are closing themes,—unless we
designate F and G also as side themes,—an argued point which
has no force here. Hereby, however, the contents are not indicated exhaustively, because several of the sentences are subject
to characteristic developments and changes, which almost serve
as independent thoughts; and the object here is but to give a
clew to finding one's way amid this profusion of figures.

The entire part bubbles over with fresh, glowing life. The
tempo "Allegro molto con brio" is absolutely applicable as a
whole, but experiences various changes amid the numerous sentences and developments. Here we find abundant opportunity
of thinking about rhythmic freedom and rhythmic steadiness,
and especially of melting together the different rhythmic gradations.

The principal theme, A—given more completely under A
and B, page 85—stands forth vividly, with emphasis on the
principal tones of measures 1, 3, 5, 7, and with intensification of
measure 3 over 1, and 7 over 5, and with its liquid movement of
eighths, beginning with measure 5. At measure 13 a new sentence seems to develop—*a:*

but it is in reality only a manifestation of the first motive, as is
shown at *b*, and measure 16. This entire part adheres rigorously
to the tempo; the passages of eighths are played fluently and
smoothly, but with emphasis (and with the very slightest delay

or accent) of the principal tones, from measure 19 to 23. Where
will this end? In measure 25 the principal motive again appears, but in the form of a question (chord of the second, departure from the key), and sustained, without movement of
eighths, broadened out, as it were, with a coda phrase,

the motive marked *ff*, the coda *pp*. Evidently that which appeared previously is broken off here; it stands still on its motive.
Here (the content fairly demands it) there must be a delay on
the first chord, and the coda must be played considerably slower.
At 77, and still more at 777, there must be a pause. (The first
and third time the pause must be greater than is indicated.)
The repetition of this passage demands a similar utterance, but a
more impressive one. Then the delay is at an end; the two following chords lead back with fresh courage and sharp intonation
to the first tempo, to which the first side theme (C) also con-
forms throughout.

The second side theme (D) assumes a different character;
it seems to beg off the past violence, and to make peace. Member for member (2 pulses, again 2, then 4) has the same content, which at the repetition becomes intensified and so expressive that one can almost hear the words. The passage must, from
the very beginning, be taken only the least trifle slower;

at any rate, in the performance of the eighths there must be a
slight delay upon every first eighth of the measure, and from
here on there must be new life; every member (*d, c, b-flat, g*), as
the very tone progression shows, must enter with a full tone, and

decrease a trifle. The mark >— placed over the notes will in-indicate this; it is, however, not Beethoven's annotation, for how could he indicate everything? The second member—*e-flat, d, c, a*—begins less emphatically than the other.

The figure of eighths at last begins again, and becomes intensified as to movement and strength up to the point marked *ff*, which restores it again to the original movement. The following, or third, side theme (E) rocks itself into gentle rest and milder movement. The little melody (*c | b, f | e*) demands a legato, with gentle emphasis on *f*, even when the same appears in the left hand; the figure of octaves in the right hand must be carried out softly and fluently, and absolutely subordinate to the melody. Its continuation (measures 8 and 9 of the passage) returns to the first movement, in which also the passage F appears, with power which is still more intensified at the repetition in sixteenths. Each time the principal tones of every measure must be made emphatic, and the close (measures 7 and 8 of the passage) must be given powerfully, although not exactly fortissimo. Here again the *ff* is intended to mean only "strong," for the utmost power is not applicable.

The first closing theme (G) should be heard softly, hovering, as it were, while the bass tones are uttered strongly; whereupon the second closing theme (H) begins with strong emphasis, and from F swings itself down in a light and fiery manner.

The second part of the Allegro brings anew the principal theme with full power. The figures of eighths which are here adjoined will bear an acceleration which might include measures 1 and 2, 3 and 4, 5 and 6, 7 and 8, 9 and 10, 11 and 12,—every two measures, however, going out again from the original tempo. This change in the tempo is adapted to the two-measure rhythmic structure of the passage, and demands at the same time intensity of power. If this sentence is thus rendered, however, with judgment, it obtains peculiar life; exaggeration would of course lead to a nervous and destructive effect.

These are followed by a "Durchführung" (thematic development) of the motive of the last closing theme. Here there is a slight delay upon every first tone of the motive, which becomes more defined where piano and decrescendo is annotated. The motive of A marked *pp* also appears very much held back, and does not assume its old tempo until it arrives at *ff*.

The second movement of the Sonata requires only a brief remark. After the principal theme in C major has passed over very gently ("con gran expressione") it seems necessary to express the side theme in A-flat major powerfully and sonorously. It is not thus annotated; indeed, we find immediately before this the *pp* written twice and the transition to A-flat marked ⟵⟩⟨⟶, and lastly *decres*. But the contents place the suggested interpretation beyond all doubt.

In regard to the *minore* of the Scherzo, the necessary points have been indicated on page 47.

F-Major Sonata, Op. 10.*

This delightful Sonata requires but few remarks. The first movement offers, immediately after the preluding measures of the principal theme and first side theme (C major), true models of Beethovenian melody. Each contains four measures occurring twice; each rises in a gentle curve, then sinks down, and therefore requires a gentle crescendo and diminuendo; each demands subordination of the accompaniment, both in the progression of sixteenths and also the quarters. Beethoven certainly had a definite idea of the expression of this accompaniment, for he not only placed legato marks over the melody, but over the accompaniment as well.

The second movement, called the Menuett, is a masterpiece in small dimensions, and requires a well-measured performance. The melody, with both voices in absolute equality, begins darkly and mysteriously (due corde would perhaps best express it), and not in the usual allegretto tempo which Beethoven has indicated. At measure 5 this double melody is joined by an upper voice, and from here on a brighter (tutte corde), though not a stronger, quality of tone might be adaptable. The entire passage must gently crescendo; it reaches its climax in measure 6, at the appoggiatura tone *E-flat*, upon which there is a slight delay; from there on, the passage sinks back into quiet. The repetition of this first part is expressed in exactly the same manner. The second part begins with two voices in imitation, which must be played thus—

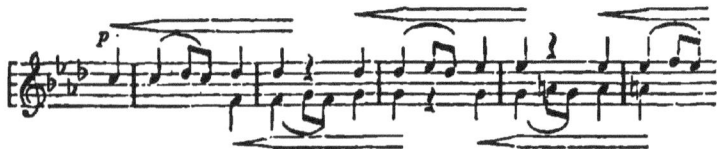

---

* Biography, Part 1. Page 164.

Beethoven's *sf* pertains more to the accompaniment.

Here the first melody appears again in higher register; and one conversant with orchestral instruments cannot resist a thought of the sweet tones of the flute whose song soars high into the ethereal heavens. Here certainly a gentle, soft performance, devoid of accent, is the most appropriate. The D-flat major passage (trio, in technical language) is one of those which exist more in the unity of the whole than in the melody, which only begins to become significant in measure 11; and even here the harmonic element is equiponderant, if not preponderant. Nevertheless, though there must be an absolutely even and quiet touch of all the voices, the melody (upper voice) must be heard a trifle above them.

Now the harmonic element begins to unfold itself in most peculiar manner, in that it slowly and most meditatively hovers through the various tone regions, spheres into which up to this time no composer for the piano had penetrated. The passage had in the beginning a deep position (*D-flat—f*). The higher tones of the same pitch (*f-f̄*) begin the repetition of the passage, but the deep tones (*D-flat—d-flat*) are struck after these, and thus represent the depth more emphatically; indeed this depth becomes personal, as it were,

in that it attains to melody (or speech). The little melodic passage must grow in intensity up to *g-flat*, tarry almost imperceptibly, then die away. Beethoven has marked three *sf*'s, and rightly; for these three tones must be made felt. These *sf*'s must, however, not be played with sharpness, but according to the thought; only very moderate power, supported by a gentle delay, is appropriate here.

Thus a melody has presented itself against the harmony, and strange to say, in the lower register. Now the harmony hovers between the tones (*f—c-flat* and *c—a-flat*), and the melody (again with flute quality) responds in a high register (*f̄-f*); the harmony then rises to its utmost possible height (*f̄-f*), and the melody rises into the highest tones (*g-flat—a*) of the present key. The violoncello is suggested here.

The last movement is marked "Presto"; and though Beethoven in his virtuosity period may have played it so, it is hardly supposable that he used this tempo later on, when he essayed to make everything intelligible. The movement is neither brilliant nor impassioned, but, rather, moody. Even the most rapid movement would not tend to give it these qualities; and its humor would become deteriorated if the presto be not taken slower.

D-Major Sonata, Op. 10.*

Full of life and spirit, this is in character the first large sonata of Beethoven's, though it is not so called.

The first Allegro develops its first principal theme from a motive of four tones,—$\bar{d}$ | $\overline{c\text{-}sharp}$, b, a,—which is also further developed. This principal subject—the first four measures—is intensified in the thesis according to movement and power, up to the last three tones, which are held back for intensification of power. The antithesis falls back into the tempo, and is repeated in a figure of eighths. The whole is based on the first motive up to the very close. For this motive Beethoven has given a hint at the very beginning.

Let us think of the first tone as made very distinct (this is brought about through the octave), the second tone—$c\text{-}sharp$—phrased to the first and shortened to an eighth, as at † (this is indicated by the staccato mark), finally the motive diminishing according to its progression ($\succ$), and we have the manner of playing this motive wherever it is found. Beethoven could not possibly indicate this everywhere. Finally the thesis is repeated, and continues for two measures; the intensification carries it on of its own accord, and the last tones demand a greater delay, without, however, coming to a satisfactory close.

The unsatisfactory close of the first leads to a second principal theme, in B minor, entirely different from the first; a plaintive tone picture which forms a first, song-like part, begins a second, which it however broadens without a close into a trans-

---

* Biography, Part I, Page 168.

ition to the first secondary subject in A major. This requires no
further description. A second secondary subject, gently and
finely constructed, like the first, follows; and in it the motive
again seeks its identity. It appears, as it were, unnoticed, in the
lower voice, mutters on in this voice, and works itself around
through different voices (of two each); here a sharper intonation of the first tone is superscribed and necessary; and lastly it
develops into a broad bass passage, increasing in intensity, bringing the entire passage to a fortissimo, and lastly pausing emphatically. Thus the broad changing tone structure is brought to a
close. Two closing themes, one agitated and one quiet (to be
played contemplatively), give repose to the close; then the motive leads back to the beginning, and from the repetition of the
first part into the second.

The Largo is a song of deep melancholy. The melody of the
first theme must not only be heard clearly above the absolutely
even and quiet, though sonorous, chords of the accompaniment,
but every tone must have the proper expression. Beethoven has
attributed so much importance to this that he finally duplicates
the melody (measures 6 and 7) in octaves. A similar emphasis
is due the melody of the second theme, where it is to be played
more legato and with finer but audible emphasis, while the accompanying figure in its deep register steals along quietly and
unassumingly with its figure of sixteenths. Finally, in the coda
the first melody (for only two measures) appears in the depths
of the bass, repeats itself, and leads on. All this must hover
over like a dark mystery; the accompaniment—first of triplets
in thirty-seconds, then of sixty-fourths—must begin like a breath,
must grow very gradually, finally appear emphatically, and, after
the indicated *forte*, fall back at once into the *piano* quality.

Pathetique Sonata, Op. 13.*

The first movement of this Sonata is marked "Allegro molto
e con brio,"—that is, with double and triple vivacity; and yet
we must avoid a hurried tempo. The performance would not be
difficult even in the most rapid tempo; but we ought not to do all
that we can do. The content demands great vivacity, and this
Beethoven has indicated as the general character; but its *pathétique* character consists not only in the breadth of the tone masses,
but also in the numerous moments which demand emphasis. We

* Biography. Part I, Page 176.

must take into consideration, also, the Grave, which introduces
the movement and reappears twice; and it would not be well to
separate too greatly the tempi of the Grave and the Allegro.
If the feeling does not deceive me (for absolute dictation cannot be given in such cases), the tempo of the Allegro ought
hardly to be four times as rapid as that of the Grave,—that four
Allegro quarters should have a trifle shorter duration than one
Grave quarter.

The Grave appears in heavy, measured rhythm; beside the
upper voice, the bass voice appears with equal significance, only
that its intensity falls more upon the first tone of the measure,
while that of the upper voice falls more upon the third quarter.
The first cadenzing figure of the upper voice should be brought
out rhythmically and strongly, while the second should be quiet
and tender.

The principal theme (page 55) comprises an opposing
theme within itself. It progresses upward in quarters, and demands, therefore, intensity of power and movement. It descends
in a broad progression of half notes. The first half-measure
chord should be a trifle held back, in order to bring out clearly
the content of this descending progression, "the lion's paw!"
That which follows returns to the first movement, and the *cres.*
seems to find interpretation in this way. Were the meaning to
be taken verbally, the whole thesis, and even the climax of the
passage ($\bar{c}$), would need to be taken piano; and then, contrary
to the tonal significance of the two halves of the passage, the
crescendo would follow, and this crescendo would lead to the
piano of the repetition. Beethoven has felt rightly, and has
made use of the word, not in a bad sense, only in an unusual
sense. How can one find room, aside from the notes, to indicate
all changes of expression? At any rate, the interpretation, as
here described, with intensification and diminution of the vibratory power repeated twice, seems to gain both in simplicity and
grandeur, and seems to be in accordance with the thought of the
whole.

It must be borne in mind that the melody of the Adagio must
not only be heard above the accompanying sixteenths (later on,
triplets of sixteenths), but must in itself be uttered in a song-like
manner, with all the intonation, crescendo and diminuendo, which
would be given to it were the hand to be used for the melody
alone. Even accomplished players neglect this point, and content themselves (forced into this habit through the technical

difficulties of newer compositions) with the former. Beethoven, however, cannot be served in so mechanical a fashion as Thalberg and his contemporaries, for with them the difficulties are not so great; but we must bring to Beethoven feeling and abandon.

G-Major Sonata, Op. 14.*

This delightful sonata requires but a few remarks; and perhaps even these few are superfluous.

Finesse and grace must guide the playing of every tone of the first movement; and the suggestions made on page 90, in regard to finished violin playing, would find most desirable demonstration here. The very first motive of six tones must be played most tenderly, absolutely legato, and with a gentle emphasis of the second tone. At its third appearance it is to be intensified somewhat, still more so the fourth time, with a slight emphasis of the *c* and a tarrying emphasis on $\bar{a}$. Added to this, the bass, as a subordinate, however, not insignificant part, must melt into the other; it is like an assenting gesture to the soulful song of the upper voice. The close of the upper voice has been marked by Beethoven thus, as at **a**,

with a legato mark for the tones of each pulse. Does it not seem, however, as though the notation of the figure as shown at **b** would give a still finer rendering? This is by no means a bold criticism of the notations of the master, but only an attempt to interpret the same more accurately. He acted wisely, to indicate the same as at **a**, and to leave for the player the fine points of interpretation which could hardly be expressed, on paper at any rate. Immediately after this, at the close of the side theme, the same notation returns

for similar tone groups, — however, in double length of tones.

* Biography, Part I, Page 170.

Here the manner of playing suggested at **b** in the preceding passage, would not be advisable; for here the song glides quietly and gently over the thrice repeated figure, so that the second tone never receives emphasis as it did before.

The dainty triplets of sixteenths (two and two marked 6) following soon after should have a light emphasis on the fourth tone.

The progressions of thirds in the side-theme form a duet, a song of two similar voices. Here the usual custom of allowing the upper voice to be intensified, and raised tenderly over the other, cannot be enforced. The two voices must warble their innocent song like birds, and the accompaniment goes along beside them. At last the thought becomes deeper, and the bass with gentle dignity forms its own melody. One never knows how far the most harmless beginning can progress, yet all remains in full unity of character with the beginning; but insight must be acquired by the player.

In the very second part the player can make use of penetrative perception. The motive, so happy at first, now begins in minor, saddened, and at measure 7 becomes involved in an excited discussion between two voices; at *f* it proceeds into the bass for the purpose of a further-reaching and more animated argument; it is a new, seriously speaking, even severe personality which here takes up the word and leads the motive which began so harmlessly, playfully, into a sphere of which it never dreamed. The after-effects are seen at the close of the passage; in vain do we await the return of the first sweet happiness.

A-flat Major Sonata Op. 26.*

In place of the usual Allegro, this Sonata has for a first movement variations of most poetic content. Beginning with the theme, and indeed throughout, every tone must be uttered soulfully, and every voice must be begun and carried through thoughtfully.

The melody of the theme, fresh as new life,

----

* Biography, Part I, Page 184.

begins at once in octaves which must fall exactly together; the three tones *a-flat* must be gently intensified; the chords of measures 3 and 4 must be uttered sonorously, but gently and with accurate simultaneous sounding of the tones. The bass, however, which carries an important melody throughout the entire movement, must be separated from the other voices by gentle intensification and staccato. Later (measures 5 to 8) it becomes legato and songlike, and with slight emphasis on the *f*. Its song reminds one of the quality of the violoncello.

In the first variation one seems to hear the interchanging song of the violoncello and the clarinet, and later (*f, a-flat, b-flat f, e-flat*) that of the flute; that is, one is reminded of the melting quality of the first, the rich tone of the second, and the airy nature of the third. This might be carried out more or less elaborately; at any rate such recollection inspires a more varied manner of playing.

The second variation places the melody first in the bass, then in a middle voice. It begins softly and darkly and becomes brightened and intensified in its progression. The melody must stand out—in measures 1 and 2 the entire left hand, in measures 3 and 4 the tones *a-fllat, a-flat, b-flat,* | *c, b-flat,* the thirty seconds, also the tones *d-flat, d-flat, c* | *f, b-flat, e-flat,* and so on. All other tones of the bass and the entire play of the right hand are subordinated to the melody, although they now and then become intensified and again decrease.

The third variation admits of a slight intensification of the tempo. It begins piano and makes a crescendo up to measure 8, the first two eighths of which are slightly held back and separated from the others by the slightest pause. The second section, from the upbeat of measure 8 to measure 16, begins like the first; like this it becomes intensified as to movement and power, and is again separated from the following by a little pause. The next twice-two measures are held back and sharply intoned, and each of the two parts separated. If the entire variation has shown a dismal, mournful character, this becomes decidedly apparent in these four measures. The next six measures form a development and must be taken at least in the first tempo, if not a little held back. Then the first part begins again with perceptible holding back of the next to the last measure.

In the fourth variation, the important tones

e-flat, a-flat, g, etc., must be lifted out, but only according to the relationship of intensity of the whole, which is originally intended to be *pp.* The tones marked *cres.*, measures 7 and 8, may be held back a little and should be played with a strong stroke. That the coda to the last variation must be played with greatest care will be felt by everyone. The melody must sing gently and persuasively, the accompaniment of sixteenths must be subordinated, while the bass in the first seven measures must give the pizzicato effect of the double bass; then, as though representing a violoncello interchanging with the double bass, it must mingle its legato with the other voices.

The third movement of the Sonata is the celebrated Funeral March on the death of a hero. Whether or not it be true that Paer's Funeral March on the death of Achilles inspired Beethoven to this composition, it certainly is a hero who is here to be laid away. For this reason the slow tempo with which this March is generally played is entirely out of keeping with its significance. Indeed, they are not old women or infirm bourgois who follow the bier! One must imagine troops, troops in arms mutilated warriors, pale with rage, whom the fallen hero has often led to victory and glory. Therefore the tempo ought to be placed at about *Allegro moderato;* and the circumstance as to whether this is the proper tempo for a soldier's march is not to be considered, for it is not such a one, but it is an ideal March, a part of a free work of art bound to no outward law. In the Trio one seems to hear the roll of the funeral drums and the sharp cry of the brasses.

Furthermore, the March moves along in four sections of four measures each. Imagine that the procession approaches from a distance. According to this it should be begun softly, and gently intensified up to the anxious chord in measure two of the fourth section. The first two sections can be played *a due corde*, but the entrance of the third (B minor) should be taken *tutte corde.* After the four sections a new one follows in which a more personal lament becomes perceptible (*pianissimo*, the *ff* to be understood according to the relationship of the *pp*), and the principal thought returns again with broader quality, now intensified (in the third from the last measure) to greatest power, and closing with powerful strokes. After the Trio, the March begins again, becomes intensified as before, must, however, not begin *pp*, but with medium strength. The coda returns to *pianissimo*.

The restlessly flowing fourth movement must by no means be played too hurriedly, in order that every voice progression can be distinctly perceived and comprehended.

Fantasie Sonata Op. 27, 1.*

This presents a series of movements without any special difficulties, technically speaking, and yet requiring careful study for poetic respresentation.

The first movement begins with the simplicity of a quiet Folk song, and retains this character throughout; the melody must rise gently above the middle voices, the bass plays thoughtfully, almost secretly, into the other parts, until it finally (part 2, measure 2) becomes more urgent, and from here on more significant.

Now a second song theme begins, simple as the first, but more rapid and stirring. The melody must not only be lifted out, but its moments must be expressed

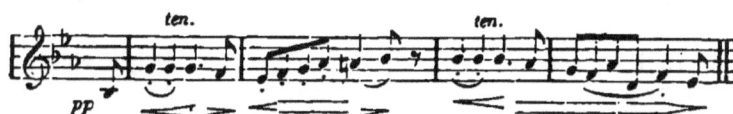

as soulfully (with stronger, but still moderated emphasis on *a*) as the hand would allow if it had only the melody to play, and not a part of the accompaniment with it. This demand becomes an absolute condition, the deeper we penetrate into Beethoven's works. The full-voiced chords of the accompaniment must be played *pianissimo*, with absolute evenness of all the tones, entirely subordinated to the melody, but increasing and diminishing with it. In order to intensify the power, the dampers must be raised (Ped.) wherever this can be done without blurring the chords or disturbing the melody (for example in measure 2). There follows (as it were a Trio) a passage marked Allegro, in which happy expectation (or recollection?) rules. The movement must not be over hurried, in order that the passage may not form too sharp a contrast to that which precedes and to the Andante which is repeated after its close.

* Biography, Part I, Page 140.

After the Andante has closed, as it were, expired, there follows a second movement, marked Allegro molto vivace.   It must
at least be taken as rapidly (or even more so) as to have its quarters about the length of the eighths in the preceding Allegro.
There is, in this movement, a hasty, restless pressing forward, full
of secrecy and suppressed passion, suddenly bursting forth.   The
first two measures hasten by softly, almost without accent, the
following two demand emphasis on the first tone of the measure;

the next two measures again remain almost without accent.   The
next four measures are taken in the same manner; at the indicated *forte* the first tones of the measure are sharply accented,
and the following ones are played less strongly.   This idea must
be kept in mind, for it has its foundation in the entire form and
content of the passage.

At the *Finale*, overhurrying of the tempo (Allegro vivace)
must be guarded against.   The content must not become indistinct for a single moment, and thorough justice must be given to
the emphatic and dignified language.

Fantasie Sonata Op. 27, 2.* †

Unless all traditions are false, this Sonata has most decided
content.   It is the echo of that which took place in Beethoven's
heart when he anticipated, or rather realized, that the bond of
love to Julia Guiccardi had been severed.   Even though this interpretation might seem somewhat uncertain, the content of the
Sonata represents that mental condition so clearly as to guide
the player's conception, passage for passage.

The first movement pictures to anyone who brings a heart to

---

* Biography, Part I, Page 130.

† More recent investigations have proven, beyond a doubt, that Beethoven's "Immortal
Beloved" was not Guilietta Guiccardi, but her cousin, the Countess Theresa of Brunswick, the
only woman whom Beethoven loved.   The interpretation of this Sonata, as Marx perceived it,
is not in accordance with the facts brought forward by Alexander Wheelock Thayer in 1879,
and confirmed by Mariam Tenger in her " Personal Reminiscences of Beethoven's ' Immortal
Beloved,' " first made known at the Beethoven festival in Bonn in 1890.

THE TRANSLATOR.

music, most decidedly a song of lamentation and self-denial. The accompaniment which unites the introduction, close, and intermediate themes, forms harplike triplets over a bass stealing along in the depths. This entire part must be played softly, with scarcely perceptible emphasis on the first tone of the triplets and with very gentle *crescendo* and *decrescendo* in the first four measures which form the introduction; after this the movement follows the rising and falling of the melody. The bass first begins to come into prominence in measures 16 to 18, and at the return of this passage rises significantly and sinks again into quiet. In measures 28 to 31 the first tone of the triplets is doubled, and therefore intensified, by a new voice (which cannot be considered as a continuation of the principal melody); from here on the triplets, as has been remarked before on page 77, attain individual significance and form, then the doubling of the melody returns. This doubling is like the entrance of a strange voice; this is especially noticeable in the last ten measures, where the first motive of the principal melody sounds up out of the deep (*G-sharp, G-sharp, G-sharp*), slightly lifted out, but not too loudly or too roughly.

It is more essential than ever that the principal melody be lifted above the accompaniment and be separated from the same. The majority of accomplished players, even, permit themselves to play melody and accompaniment, where they fall together in octaves,

with a flat hand and with absolute evenness of intensity. This deprives the melody of the prominence due to it, and even gives it a sense of incompleteness, when it falls together with the accompaniment. It must stand out independently, but with great gentleness. Perhaps at the close, measures 14 to 11 from the end, an exception might be made, and the gradually vanishing song might be allowed to melt away with the same intensity as the accompaniment.

The song begins very softly, but at the return of the beginning in F-sharp minor it takes on a brighter hue and assumes greater intensity. It will be clearly seen that the melody must be played as expressively, with increase and decrease of power as though the hand had nothing else but this to play.

This song of lament is followed by a second movement, marked Allegretto, after which comes the stormy, impassioned Finale. The latter is generally played more or less accurately by pianists, for it is generally considered as the exact opposite of the lamentation, both as pourings forth of a soul strung to its utmost. The second movement, however, awakens doubt, and is misunderstood, and therefore misinterpreted by the majority of players. This doubt received strongest expression in the excellent pianist, composer, and teacher, Louis Berger, who declared that this movement disturbed the unity of the Sonata, and that it must needs be left out. He further stated that the fact that a C-sharp minor movement followed a C-sharp minor movement, would be only the slightest objection to this plan. Indeed, if this second movement is only played as Allegretto, with the usual gradations of expression, we might readily arrive at the mood of a Vienna Waltz, and might readily be tempted to agree with the venerable Berger. But here again it is seen how essential it is to look beyond the notes into the inspiration which caused the composer to write thus.

The song of lament is a very general lyric effusion, but it is a real moment out of the life of a definite person — in this case Beethoven, who laments that he must part from his love. The necessity of parting, this determined personal thought, is not expressed in the song; that is the content of the second movement. The farewell words, "O think of me! I think of thee! Farewell, farewell . . . . forever!" these ever-recurring parting words of lovers seem to be heard distinctly out of the tones. One who cannot hear those words should think them, and one who cannot think them should lay aside the Sonata, it is not written for him.

Therefore the indicated tempo of the movement is above all essential — the parting one turns away, not, however, without vivid mental agitation. For this reason, even tempo throughout would be a caricature; it would presuppose evenness of feeling, whereas in parting everything wavers, especially in the first moments; for self-control can only be acquired gradually. The beginning should be played lively, but even at the third and fourth tones there should be a slight delay, and a longer one at the first rest. The repetition of the thought, "O think of me" (*g-flat* | *f, e-flat,* | *a-flat*), with the following rests, should be played with still more lingering, for the feeling is now awakened, the thought has now become a consciousness. The changed repetition of the passage (*d-flat,* | *d-flat, c, b-flat,* | *b-flat, c-flat*) begins to acquire fluent speech, but with hesitation after *c-flat* and *a-flat* where before rests were required; the close hesitates. The second part follows in more closed and even tempo, hurrying by in the first four measures, holding back in the two following, and tarrying long in the *e-flat.* This hesitation, this unsteadiness of the anxious soul must be understood and expressed through the tones, expressed with the language of innermost feeling which penetrates without words from heart to heart.

Who can know of the pictures which hover over the recollection in the Trio,—images which once more beckon from the past, and which waft words of comfort on the breath of the tones. One must hear with the soul, not alone with the physical ears; one must feel, not simply count, the pulses; must respond to the soul of the poet instead of merely obeying the prescribed tempo and the arithmetical problem.

Now, at length, the Finale becomes intelligible. One does not perish at once; still less does the longed-for and hoped-for happiness become a reality—and yet life must continue. One must live on amid the storm of unhappy and restless existence, must wear out his last strength in the violence of desire and with a lamentation which reaches about in vain. That is the content of the Finale; once before, in the F-minor Sonata Op. 2, Beethoven found no other relief for inner soul-life.

D-Major Sonata Op. 28.*

"A noble thought attracts noble men;" this might be said of this Sonata, with only a slight change in the words of the poet. A simple, grand, experienced soul is here represented, capable of the greatest emotions. The player must be able to absorb this greatness and depth, and to express it freely. There is here no opportunity for violent and sharp contrasts; all is developed gradually and quietly, and therein is manifested the power and grandeur. Never has ignorance exposed itself more absurdly than in giving this Sonata (who knows in whose brain the idea originated?) the name "Pastoral Sonata." This name evidently has reference to the first theme of the Finale. One might as well call Solon or Plato a writer!

The first Allegro develops its principal theme (given on page

* Biography, Part I, Page 185.

64) quietly for ten measures; the upper voices progress downward quietly, but rhythmically significant (with emphasis on the
principal tones of measures 5 and 6), and rise with the same gentleness; the melody must be raised slightly above the middle
voices. It has been said before, on page 64, that the bass in progression of quarters does not pulse along without significance;
its strokes increase from *piano* for four measures, decrease for
two ·measures, then increase again. The theme is repeated, but
more impressively and with finer coloring. The quarters in the
bass now resound an octave higher, and therefore come to the
ear more vividly. The upper voices also return in a higher octave (the melody in a finer tone register) and in broader harmony; hereby the tenor especially becomes more individualized,
and attains individual song, the first tone of which must stand
out, the following four (*f-sharp, g, b, e,*) swelling out of the *piano*,
the last three vanishing away. At first the melody, bass, and
middle voices were to be distinguished, now upper and tenor
melody, bass, and middle voices which join the others, are to be
perceived.

These twice-ten measures have not proven exhaustive, for
there follows a second principal theme of eight measures, related
to the first, and with a bass continuing its pulsations, closing with
four measures of coda. This, however, is not like the first, but
simply related to it; the first two measures press more actively
beyond the original tempo, which had remained steady throughout the first theme, and after these measures the original tempo
returns, up to the repetition of the introductory figure of eighths
which again raises itself in movement and intensity. The repetition demands a similar interpretation of course, but with greater
intensification of the melody, which is now doubled.

Now the side theme quietly begins (*b, a, a, g-sharp, b, d*) in four
and four measures in the first tempo. It is repeated with figuration of eighths; and here the progression demands more activity,
more intense tempo, but with well-balanced restraint. It seems
feasible in this passage

to hasten the groups marked *a* a little, but to hold back slightly those marked *b*—all so gradually, however, that the unity of the whole will not be disturbed. Thus the progression of eighths becomes gradually more active, and ·returns to the tempo in the last two measures. The following passage in quarters is related to this.

In the following passage of eighths the intensity of movement must grow gently for 14 measures, just as the preceding; it must decrease with the descending tones, then increase again up to the resting chord (*c-sharp—e—a—e*) in broad harmony, the second (*f-sharp—a—d-sharp*) still stronger, even sharply uttered—and both a little held back. In the figures of triplets and sixteenths, the first two swing rapidly down from a strong beginning, the third is held back. Then the crescendo begins again, but with greater intensity and rises to great power on the half-note chord (*c-sharp—e—a*) and on the following (*f-sharp—d-sharp—a*) to fortissimo, whereupon it again returns to moderation. The closing theme is like the principal theme in intensity and tempo.

For the second part, let it be observed that the frequent *sforzatos* should not be exaggerated, but that they should be measured according to the existing intensity—especially in the upper register. The entire development over the bass tone *F-sharp*, in which the melody lies in the next to lowest, and later in the lowest voice, must from the beginning be planned for an entire vanishing away; and finally, the major chord *f-sharp—a-sharp—c-sharp* must be continued in grand repose, gradually growing slower, sinking, as it were, into the depths of tone life. In the same sense the close of the whole must gradually vanish away. Here let the poetic player observe the rising melodic progression in the last melodic member,

which places the up-beat upon $\bar{a}$, then upon $\bar{d}$, upon $\bar{f}$-sharp, upon $\bar{a}$, and finally—but here this melody vanishes—rises to $\bar{d}$. It is an exuberance which can only be appreciated by a singer. Let the pianist perceive what there is for him to do.

An Andante follows, which seems to have the character of an old ballad. The bass plays a harplike accompaniment, the upper voices pass quietly over the same; the second quarter, measure 1 and 5 must be gently emphasized. The second part, up to the repetition of the principal thought, requires stronger intonation.

The Trio (D major) is marked *p* by Beethoven. The annotation is very applicable to the whole passage, but of course does not preclude the required gradations of the individual moments. This gradation is at once presented in the contrast of the four-voiced chords, and the following solo-figures; the former must resound with resonance, though not strongly, as though uttered by soft wind instruments (clarinets, fagotti), while the solos must enter gracefully between them.

The other parts of the Sonata require no further remarks for their interpretation.

G-Major Sonata, Op. 31.

This Sonata, one of the happiest moments of Beethoven's life, though presenting no technical difficulties, requires, for an expressive interpretation, an absolutely loose hand, ready for all the fine points of execution.

The entire first movement is pervaded by a mood, the representation of which seems to require no advice except to interpret the notes and to let freedom reign throughout. Even these few serious words seem to limp laboriously after the brightness of the tone poem!

The lightness and happy mood of the first movement is manifest in the shortness of the phrases, in the half playful, half dreamy stops and pauses, which we will here indicate by numbers. At 1 the upper voice steps forward with a sixteenth, and therefore becomes more impressive, but still without violence or particular significance. Beethoven has marked the same *ff*.* We understand that he means by this not special strength, but energy as compared with the adjacent parts; at any rate, here the *ff* cannot be given the intensity which we are accustomed to associate with this sign. After this beginning, the melody runs along easily and lightly. For 2 and 3, Beethoven himself has written *p*; for 4 he has marked *f*. In the last phrase, the bass might come somewhat hesitatingly after the right hand, and the pause after 4 might be lengthened a trifle. Five has the first movement; a slight prolonging of the pause after it would make the close of the passage more emphatic.

The subject is repeated in F major. The first phrase returns

---

* Possibly this should be only *f*, as at the repetition.

/

as 6; 7 is marked *p*, as was 2 before; 8 with *f*, which, however, can only mean *piu forte* here; 9 and 10 are to be taken like 4 and 5; 11 and 12 likewise, only 11 somewhat stronger. The long passage of sixteenths cannot be played without accelerating the tempo, especially in the last five measures. The subject is repeated as at 1, and appears again in the first tempo; its last phrases before the sixteenths begin hesitatingly, and lessen the movement.

A similar interpretation should be given to the coda. Especially must the sixteenth triplets (first turn, then arpeggio) be spared any impetuosity or haste—in fact they ought rather to be held back. It is strange but comprehensible that even skilled players often deal so inconsiderately with this simple and frequently applied figure of the doppelschlag, this graceful embellishment of the principal tone. .

The Adagio grazioso, the second movement of the Sonata, might really be called Italian—not that it is an echo of Rossini's or other Italian works, but rather an ideal representation of all the sweetness, *abandon*, and vivacity which we can conceive of as united under Hesperia's heavens. Beethoven accomplished here (for the Sonatas Op. 31 were written in 1802–3) what Rossini strove to attain, and in his happiest moments did attain—this union of playfulness and most graceful coquetry. The player must be filled with this sentiment; the trills of the upper voice must be executed with the utmost fluttering quickness, with absolute equality of motion or of retard; they must grow from a *pianissimo* into an increased intensity;* but when these same trills appear in the left hand, they must roll along in a subdued quality of tone. The small figures must now be hurried, now delayed in the daintiest manner, in order to express the grace and vivacity of the mood. On the other hand, the quintolets toward the end of the principal theme require an evenness and steadiness of tone. More cannot be said in words.

D-Minor Sonata Op. 31.†

This deep, thoughtful work presents to the player in the very beginning of the first movement a mystery, upon the solution of which the success of the entire movement depends. After a Largo of two measures there begins an entirely new Allegro

passage, continuing for three measures and closing in the fourth
with an Adagio. The Largo passage of two measures then repeats itself, and the Allegro passage (somewhat changed) reappears and continues to the end of the first part. Were we to
consider the Largo as introductory, what then is the significance
of this Allegro of three measures, which cannot possibly develop
its thought in so narrow a space, and only to yield it up in the
Adagio? What means this wandering back and forth from the
Largo to the Allegro, then again to the Largo, and again to the
Allegro? If, furthermore, the Allegro passages are taken too
rapidly at the beginning, perhaps as they should be taken later
on (and thus we have frequent opportunity of hearing them,
especially in the concert room), the mystery becomes deeper
and more perplexing. We must penetrate deeper.

The Largo is the introduction, a thought which has not yet
assumed form. A second representation, the Allegro, is awakened, and also cannot complete itself as yet. The Largo is really
only a single chord, which slowly manifests itself; the first six
arpeggio tones begin slowly and follow in accelerated movement
which rests on the *a*, moves reluctantly through $\bar{c}^e$ and $\bar{e}$ to $\bar{a}$,
and, according to Beethoven's annotation, rests there for a time.
But the Allegro is also only an introduction without completion
or satisfaction. It cannot possibly have a steady tempo; this is
indicated by the "Adagio" over the fourth measure. It has in
itself no steadiness. The passage,

must, above all, be emphasized ◼, ◼, and ―, and must be more
and more held back under 1, up to the Adagio of the fourth
measure, while at 2 it must press forward; not only its own decided character but the further development requires this wavering motion.

The Largo returns again, likewise the Allegro. Up to measure 5 it has the same character as before, only more excited, and
measures 3 and 4 require an emphasis and delay on the second
and fourth quarters. At measure 5 the movement proceeds with
more determination, and with decided accent on the first and
third quarters, up to the *sf.* marks, which indicate a retard upon

the fourth quarter notes, but again pressing forward from measure 10 to measure 21, measures 17 and 18,

seem to mutter at the last uprising, with a medium-strong dismal tone in the middle register, and with a delay and intensification upon the last pulse. It is to be observed that up to measure 19 all eighth notes are laboriously phrased together in twos, and only in measure 19 begin to appear in the ordinary and more convenient form of four in a group. This manner of writing indicates short and interrupted execution of the eighths.

Now for the recapitulation: All that has been considered thus far, up to measure 21, is introduction to the passage which begins at measure 21; it is still incomplete, is only about to be, and places two absolutely opposite motives side by side. This struggle, this indecision, must find expression, and, therefore, no definite tempo is possible, nor can there be an abrupt entrance of the Allegro. As yet nothing exists, nothing is determined or decided, all is uncertain, wavering, interrogative; therefore all is excited, strained to the utmost for that which is to come.

At measure 21 the principal theme enters, and at once with absolute decision, therefore in firm and lively tempo, and with power. Thereby begins, then, the first part of the Allegro. The principal theme is laid out in broad sections of four and four measures. Its first motive (two measures) is that of the Largo, but is now to be played with power; this is followed by the counter theme, consisting of a motive of a plaintive character (likewise of two measures), and marked especially with *p*, as the first was with *f*. The first motive is the ruling one; but both must be firmly united, regardless of their opposite character, and must be emphasized and diminished thus:

This section repeats itself, beginning with E; then the first member (the Largo motive) repeats itself five times in F, G♯, A, B, c,
while the second member manifests itself only through a single
tone uttered after the others. These single tones are marked
sf; they must be played impressively, but not sharply (as is often
the case with high tones), in order not to be subordinate.

It has been stated above that the tempo must be firm. This
is not to be interpreted as a sameness of motion, but a determined development of rhythm, and thereby a most comprehensive rounding off of the single rhythmic parts. The broadness
of the development demands this, but at the same time, the passionate pressing forward of the passage demands acceleration.
Both demands can be united through strong intensification of
the rhythmic members. Thus the first sections (of four and four
measures) must remain firmly and grandly in the tempo, but the
following five (of two measures each) and the coda (of two measures each) must stand out with slow and steady movement. The
pressing forward of the principal theme is demanded the more,
as it does not come to a real close—therefore remains in motion.

Now follows the side theme, and this is formed from the
Allegro motive of the introduction. Hereby is proven what has
been said before of the content and thought of the introduction.
This side theme is, of course, formed naturally, according to the
thought of its motive. It is marked by Beethoven with *p* and
agitato ; its almost breathless restlessness represents it as the
most absolute opposite of the principal theme. The tempo in
the side theme can be only unsteady. It also begins in two sections of four measures each.

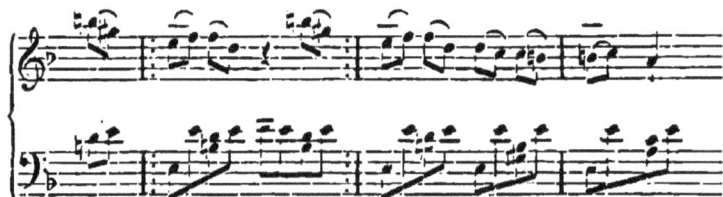

The very first measure, however, after a hasty intonation of
the first pulse, must hurry its first four eighths, and at the third
pulse hold back a little; the same is·required in the second
measure. The third presses forward, but the beginning of the

fourth is again delayed. The second section requires a similar performance. From here on the restlessness and movement increase, and at the discontinuation of the accompaniment, the melody moves strongly downward, with emphasis on all first eighths, finally strengthened by the bass.

The following two chords require full vibratory power, and combined with it a very significant holding back, especially on the second chord (*d, f, b-flat*), whereupon the quarters | *a, g♯* | a, follow with considerable moderation, and more in the prescribed tempo. These two chords are the climax of motion and power of the entire work; they must be grasped in a lionlike manner, and must sound out with power. They repeat themselves with their train in the higher octave, and again in the second higher octave, with further melodic development, up to the close on A. This climax motive moderates its power at every repetition, and gradually returns to the first movement, or nearly to the same. The six measures, beginning with the closing A, are again held back, especially at every advance of the bass.

With the beginning of the passage of eighths, the movement grows again to the absolute restoration of the first tempo. The close has been determined from the beginning. The passage of eighths, moreover, begins softly and grows (as is marked) to full power in the closing theme. The *ff* marked at the beginning indicates only a strong *sforzato* for the advancing *discantus*. The slow tones leading back into the beginning, and also forward to the second part, require no interpretation.

The second part brings first again the Largo motive in triple repetition and further development. The little notes must be played with a light, quick toss, but the large ones with a holding back. This is, then, the second representation of the motive out of which the principal theme has grown.. Has it no further determination than to serve as introduction? Not thus far. It appears, however, at the close of the part, and here it develops into an expressive recitative; the harmonic sounds become speech.

In closing, let it be impressed upon the player that the tempo of the Finale must not be taken too rapidly. Players frequently make it a Vienna waltz, or an Étude. It is nothing of the kind; indeed, it is a most thoughtful, expressive movement, permeated with desire, and excited up to agitation of feeling and tone waves, but like the entire Sonata, full of inner emotion and free from all over-haste.

E-flat Major Sonata, Op. 31.

Poetically thoughtful, yet full of playfulness, and both in constant interchange, the tone play is like a wood-inclosed meadow over which now the sun casts light spots, now the passing clouds and slender bushes cast fleeting shadows.   Both, lights and shadows, must be in the hand of the player, but finally high spirited mirth must rule.

The first Allegro begins its principal theme with a thoughtful question, and as though in thought, lets a passage of chords follow, repeats the same—and all this in a tempo not yet established, as though it were impeded by reflection.   Three more spirited measures follow as a close to the preceding, and as an introduction to that which is to come.   However, they only lead back to the question which appears now in higher regions, hovers down an octave, drawing after it an antithesis, into a second lower octave, and finishes in the very first middle register.   This fastidious hovering through tone regions is characteristic.   Beethoven delights in hovering like a bee over all the flowers which yield material for honey, in tasting them individually; but seldom has this characteristic become so manifest as in this movement.   The player must conceive of this, and must secure from every tone region a peculiar quality of tone—a dusky quality from the lowest, brightness and tenderness from the highest, and speech from the intermediate.

From the second close the tempo stands, for the present, firmly established.   Still the question hovers playfully up and down, and a firmer passage, somewhat more spirited but steady in movement, leads again to the question which now resounds so anxiously, almost painfully.   The side theme, with all attached thereto, with all its finely agitated song, remains true to the tempo, while the closing theme returns to the question and its hesitation.   The second and third parts carry out the preceding still further, and repeat portions of the same.   Hereby the execution is determined.

Now follows the Scherzo.   The octave passage, measures 9 to 17, is a pure "parlando," as though stolen from some opera bouffe.   One hears the tones and seems to hear the words— who knows what they say!   Is it, perhaps, a Rossinian buffoon that is talking?   Is it Antonio from Mozart's Cosi fan tutte? One who has ever had the pleasure of hearing Sontag—not the Countess Rossi with her noble passions, but Henrietta Sontag—

in the "Barber of Seville," or else the first of all buffoons, Spit-zeder, can comprehend this Beethovenian verse; and one who can represent to himself this absolute freedom of speech and mischievous fineness of humor knows best how to interpret this Beethoven Scherzo. The stream of tones rolls on, and a recollection of what has been said before suffices for the entire movement.

If the Scherzo was playful, certainly the Presto Finale (after a quiet Menuett which takes the place of an Adagio) is positively frivolous, especially after the fine, lightly passing first principal theme, the mirthful accents of the second, and the hurried flight (accelerated movement, smooth connection) of the third, which again seems to have escaped from some opera bouffe. It is remarkable that these suggestions of Italy are found at a time when nothing was known of Rossini, at least by Beethoven. Later he was to be driven away from the Viennese by the foreign element; however, he never showed a foreign spirit even in the G-major Sonata; besides all the playfulness and all the southern sweetness, German tenderness and ideality prevailed. One who cannot see both sides, and who does not know how to unite them, cannot do justice to this Sonata. Fleeting playfulness must be accompanied by tenderness, seriousness, by caprice. The way of doing both has been shown.

C-Major Sonata Op. 53.*

This Sonata belongs preëminently into the region of tone play; indeed, were it to be measured according to the difficulties which it presents, and according to the brilliancy of execution offered therein, one might be tempted to call it a bravoura piece. However, beyond all this brilliancy there rises a spiritual idea of which tone play knows very little. Nevertheless, apart from the technical difficulties, the performance involves no particular obstacles and requires few remarks. Indeed, even the technical difficulties are not altogether too great for a well trained pianist.

This Sonata consists of but two movements. Between them there appears an Adagio molto, but it is not an independent movement; it is simply (as the superscription declares) an introduction to the Finale.

The first movement, Allegro con brio, betrays at once the impatience of hands that are eager to play. In the *pianissimo*

* Biography. Part I. Page 179.

and in the deeper tone regions, the rapid motion of the eighths begins and becomes intensified up to the first pulse of the third measure, not very greatly, but perceptibly, and with absolute evenness of touch and movement, bringing a little stress upon the first pulse of the third measure. The fourth measure is only a refined echo of the third. The second section requires a similar utterance; it is formed like the first, but with a more elaborate close, and requires a little retardation of motion on the *decres.*

These two sections, which form the thesis of the principal theme, designated from each other by restless sixteenths, are carried with a light hand to the dominant of E major, and are there made firm and settled. The transition to the side theme is manifested rather hesitatingly (four measures before the side theme), and the player must make this felt through a slight holding back. This secondary or side theme, then, rocks itself in the shining light of its beautiful tone character; it should be held back a little, even there where the beautiful triplet figure is surrounded by a melody. The passage (beginning with the indicated *f*) returns to the original tempo, which continues to assert itself up to the quarter and eighth figure of the closing theme, where it is again held back a little, especially on the quarter notes.

The transitional passage, called "Introduzione," is a thoughtful Adagio which lays a slight emphasis on the third and sixth eighths (the first marked ten.), but hesitating in the subsequent measures and in the chord progressions. When finally these distracted phrases in measure 9 at the *rinforzando* melt together into a solid melody, one seems to hear one of those 'cello melodies which Beethoven knows so well how to make impressive in sound and content. If unable to recall any such melody character, the performance must at least make the thought of the passage impressive (especially in the first measure, to which the simile had reference) through intonation of the first eighth and of the two others marked *sf. sf.*, and this united in the syncopation and combined with a resonant quality of tone in the lower voices.

In the Finale, with its childlike, playful principal theme, exaggeration of the tempo must be guarded against. The superscription Allegretto moderato points to moderation; the beautiful principal theme demands the same; but also the two side themes, the first in A minor in triplets of sixteenths, and the second in C minor, urge to moderation, so that they can enter

characteristically. Both of these themes appear in three- and
four-fold octaves,

with impetuously beating power (it is marked *f* and *sempre f*).
Every stroke on the keys should be heard like the stroke of a
hammer. The fingers might hasten, but the listener would not
comprehend readily. Added to this is the circumstance that the
first side theme requires four intensifications,

with emphasis and a slight delay upon the last tone of the intensification. This is followed by six tones, beating with equal
strength, but the seventh again held a little. Finally the second
side theme (eight measures) places against the principal melody
a counter theme in triplets of sixteenths which may also be
called characteristic;

and the coda, this beating *gg | gggg | c*, demands emphasis for
every stroke. All this verifies the conclusion that the more
weighty the content the less can haste be employed. To the
impatient hastener the coda Prestissimo will then be a boon.

F Minor Sonata Op. 57.*

The Sonata in F minor leads us into higher regions than the
sonatas considered thus far. Something of this has evidently
come into the head of some piano hero or attentively listening

*Biography, Part II, Page 26.

music dealer, and immediately he has attached the appellation
"appassionata" to the Sonata. It is about as significant as to
call Hannibal or Napoleon a very brave warrior. Beethoven has
written very many impassioned sonatas, and of most varied content; however, he never named one according to so indeterminate
a quality. Let us discard this name and proceed to the work
itself.

One characteristic becomes noticeable at once — the tone picture is, from beginning to end, wrapped as it were in darkness.
They are not definitely defined figures moving along, which make
themselves tangibly manifest in firm outlines — all has rather the
nature of phantoms which darkly hover past, intangible as the air
into which they evaporate as soon as we approach them and attempt to hold them. Can the whole be a phantom picture of an
anxious night? For that, it manifests too great a conclusiveness.
Is it a vision such as seems to have escaped from the lower world?
This cannot be traced out according to laws of reason; but art,
the work of art, does not belong to reason, and is not born of
reason; it is a child of fantasy and belongs to it alone. It is,
however, not the fetterless and aimlessly wavering fantasy from
which this tone poem has come forth; but it is that activity of
the creative power which has given to reason, that eternal guide,
determined and ideal power. To solve such problems in the
realm of pure music was Beethoven's peculiar calling.

Whoever cannot find thought and faith for this cannot master
this work; for him the F-minor Sonata is nothing but a lesson in
technical skill. Perhaps he will confine himself only to playing
the Finale—as it has been heard in more than one Berlin concert,
by various natives, virtuosos, and teachers; that is like sawing
off Niobe's head and bust and placing the rest on a pedestal.
Now for analysis:

The first Allegro assai, and in it the very first principal theme
establishes the character of the entire tone poem. In hollow
double octaves this theme (page 49) hovers along with long
steps, softly closing, or, one might say, hesitating in a quivering,
interrogative trill. It has already been stated on page 49 that
the remote lower voice should accompany the upper still more
softly and like a shadow. After this close there is a prolonged
pause, followed by a repetition of the upper half step. Each
time the beginning tone (first *c*, then *d-flat*) should be imperceptibly delayed; in the second measure there should be a slight
accellerando toward the highest tone, and again a slight delay

on the first tone of the third measure. The little closing figure
is repeated, and again repeated; and in the intervening interval,
the mysterious, lonely

three times repeated presses up out of the dark depths, very
softly, hesitatingly, mysteriously—a warning—wherefrom? The
upper voices have long echoed this, as one returns an anxious,
unanswerable question to the inquirer.

All wavers uncertainly and unsteadily, anxiously. Now the
upper voice liberates itself with' great power (page 36); like a
cry of terror it plunges in scalloped motion with winged speed,
down into the depths, then again up into the heights; now it
seems to plunge in as though to assert itself; and still the last
chord vibrates on softly, and remains stationary as though fettered, as though awaiting final expiration.

The first theme appears again very softly, but torn at the very
third tone by the sudden and yelling cry of the harmony ($f\!f$
marked immediately after a $p\!p$); and immediately again progressing softly (marked p). -Thus fear cries out and storms
after it has been long enough denied expression of sound. Or is
it something unknown or strange which reaches darkly into the
quiet progression of this passage? Three times this thunderclap
strikes into this quiet strain.

Such hard and abrupt opposites are seldom found in Beethoven, who does not love skips and departures, but seeks quiet development, as does law in the organic and spiritual world. To
what regions do these abrupt changes refer us? Let the player
solve that, and let him have courage and power to do so. The
interrogative closing formula which appeared at the very beginning (measure 3) also returns twice; from here on we soar into
other regions, to other pictures. "Soar" is not an arbitrary expression; it is the only suitable one for the diving down of the
leading over theme (Ueberleitungssatz), which from the very first
point of entrance constantly moves over to the uncertain last
eighths, and only has the quietly remaining bass as a certain
foundation under it, and that only in restlessly pulsing strokes.

This bass, wavering back and forth in deepest register, rustles
quietly on; and over it, out of the lowest depths, then raised into

a comforting height, there resounds the first firmly-built song—a gentle, exalted song of prophecy, yea, of confidence. It vibrates over the restless depths, as though over the comfortless night of Tartarus out of which we come; later, as a song from Elysium. How terrible for the eternally condemned is this proximity to the blessed fields—this combination which the Greek, cold as his marble, has invented and handed down.

Beethoven has followed him, but not too far. For this song the interpreter must let his tenderest fingers pass over the keys; everything must be "dolce," as Beethoven has superscribed, and with scarcely audible intonation—only as much as is indispensable for rhythmic distinctness. This deep song—the first side theme—repeats itself in high register, but only partially; then it hesitates painfully, trembles forward (each one of the trills sharper than the preceding), and precipitates itself in a broad downward progression into the lower depths. Here, in the hard rolling of powerless, fettered wrath, a second side theme struggles, and after it a closing theme, both in A-flat minor. It is not advisable to analyze farther, each one must see for himself how wrath and complaint, fetter and flight, interchange.

This is the first part. He who has given himself up to the representations which this has awakened requires no further advice for interpretation; to him all these pictures become embodied amid the many gradations of intensity which one can never superscribe. That which has been established in the first part attains a complete and distinct existence in the second part. First the principal theme appears again, but more firmly, and in single, not double, octaves, then against a harmony. Hereby the figure which before has only been a hovering melody has become firm; now it raises itself strongly out of the depths to the middle, and from there to the height of the tone system. The accompanying harmony appears first in sextolets (four groups of six, it is $\frac{12}{8}$ measure) then in quintolets (five instead of six) which laboriously wind themselves downward. This explains the rendering of the melody (strong and firm) and of the accompaniment. All the following requires no further guide. The greatest intensity in the passage marked *ff*, the most daring sweep of the ascending and descending sextolets before the "Piu Allegro"—all this solves itself as soon as the preceding has been comprehended. But to the "vandal they are stones."

The second movement of the Sonata is an Andante with variations. It has been observed in the A-flat Major Sonata Op. 12, that variations in the greater works of Beethoven are not only figurations, but they generally carry a deeper sense within themselves. It is essential, therefore, to go to them with sentiment and thought, and not only with fingers. Here the theme appears in a low register, and is quiet and gentle ("piano e dolce"). The melody at first scarcely progresses, so that in measures 4 and 5, even the progression of a fourth gives significance and makes the ascent in the second part (the theme is a two-part song-form), from *a-flat* to *d-flat* and from *f* to *a-flat* seem like an impassioned ascent, very like a prayer which winds itself with fervor out of the deep (De profundis clamavi ad te). Combined with this, the bass in the deepest sense pursues its own way; it is not a principal voice, nor a second important voice (if upper and lower voice are to be personified), but it is a most worthy accompaniment to the principal voice. The performer must execute the whole movement with the utmost calmness, and with absolute precision of all the simultaneously uttered voices. The upper voice requires but the slightest lifting above the others; the bass, however, must stand out, especially in measure 3, in the progression to the great *A-flat* and its postlude, measures 4 and 8. The above cited ascents demand intensification, but the movement must remain the same.

The first variation is, as it were, an elucidation of the theme; in the first part the bass hovers, as it were, after the chorus of the other voices, in syncopated form; the second part, however, aspires to higher realms. It is still a prayer out of the depths, shadowlike in the first part, in the second it anxiously ventures upward. For theme and first variation the "due corde" would be applicable.

In a more comforting manner does the second variation rise in the middle tone region, where gentle song lives. The melody melts together with the middle voices into harplike, mild figuration; the bass leads its melody quietly and gently against this. Where before the "due corde" was applicable, the "tutte corde," suggestive of greater resonance, would here apply; it must, however, be taken very quietly throughout the entire measure.

To an accompaniment of harp whisperings the third variation enters in the register of tenderest tones, then the harplike accompaniment lays itself over the melody. The movement finally turns back to the original tone position, hovering up and down until it reaches the last chord, which, however, is not a closing chord. The movement does not close, but leads over to the

Finale. Whoever has comprehended the character and content
of the different tone regions requires no further guidance. The
contents are very simple and comprehensible, for Beethoven has
given the most important annotations. It must be remembered,
however, that the indicated *sf* and *ff* must constantly (especially
in the high positions) be graded according to the significance of
the passage in which they appear. They are entirely different
from the sharp contrasts in the first Allegro, which there essential to the meaning of the whole.

The Finale rushes along like a night storm, and according to
tradition, it was conceived by Beethoven on a stormy night. It
is possible that the outward storm may have given to the tone
poet the last revelation or decision, but certainly the storm had
been in his breast before the outward storm was perceived. He
who has seen the story which the first movement revealed, who
has sought refuge in the uprising and expiring De profundis, *his*
life is indeed storm. And if he be a man like Beethoven, mild
and good at heart, undaunted and defiant in the bluster of threatening misfortune, he will sing, courageously and loudly,

> 'Gainst snow, 'gainst rain, the storm to breast,
> On, on, still on, nor pause nor rest.

This, then, approximately (for all can by no means be explained),
is the thought which the player must be able to realize. The
chord which did not close the preceding passage, but ended it,
after a long pause resounds in sharp strokes and firmly marked
rhythmic attacks. And now, after a pause of expectation, the
storm again begins to raise its dark wings very softly in the
upper realms, as possibly everyone has heard it in the highest
summits of the woods, before it seizes the crowns and shatters
the trunks of the oaks. But it is not intended to depict a picture of nature; it is a storm of the soul, which only for a moment
might be compared to the former.

Smoothly and softly the flight of tones begins,

very legato, without accent, and the last time phrased off abruptly.
This flight rolls on ever deeper, the intensity increases, becomes
very strong, growls down in the depths, then becomes more subdued and quiet, and pauses. The storm passage rushes on,

this is the nature and form of its air waves, in which Czerny (page 89) supposed himself to have been transported to the shores of the sea. Deep into the on-rolling vibration, the "Wanderer's Night Song"

resounds, calling and struggling through the gust of wind which sweeps away the last word—the bass can scarcely point out the lost close. The second song continues more firmly amid the roar; the storm rages on, covers all with its breath and long wings; and the side theme is not entirely released

from its anxious haste.

All this, and much more that is beyond description, must be made recognizable in the interpretation In order that this (not technical execution, but representation) may be possible, Beethoven has carefully added to the direction "Allegro," a "Ma non troppo." To the strange and unexpectedly following "Presto." which sounds like a decided "Forward!" I should like to add a "Ma non troppo" in order that every eighth stroke may come out hammerlike—however, by no means noisily (it is an inner decision and marked *p*), and that it may be perceived as stroke and not as vibration. The last part in sixteenths, on the other hand, may speed on, unbridled, like the storm.

Les Adieux, Sonata Op. 81 a.*

The content of this Sonata ,s expressed in the title and in
each of the three movements marked with the words Les adieux,
L'absence, Le retour, which might be translated into Farewell,
Absence, The Return. That they are moments from the life of a
pair of lovers is presupposed.† The composition itself also furnishes proof of this, for in the first and third movements a duet
form rules throughout, namely, two voices-going with and against
each other, one deeper and one higher. Casually, at the end of
the first theme, the two voices receive support and become two
pairs of voices; this, however, in no wise changes the conception
before named. Music requires completeness of harmony and
can therefore be satisfied with single voices for only a short time.
The harmony might be a secondary consideration, and that is
often the case here, and each time with significance. It was
certainly ideally thought out by Beethoven to allow (in the passage cited on page 75) each one of the duetting voices to complete its own harmony; for not only should the outward form of
a duet be depicted, but the living content should be expressed
artistically. In order to interpret fully this tone poem, one of the
tenderest and deepest, the interpreter must have become thoroughly conversant and must have filled his heart with these three
moments of life.

The introduction (Adagio) expresses in its first tones the
"Farewell!" It is in the mild E-flat major, but even in the third
pulse the addition of the bass draws it down into the cold C-
minor key. This ominous, decisive basstone demands emphasis,
and as especial expansive power is not applicable here, there
must be a short pause instead. The mood of the following measures can be felt by everyone, but we must farther comprehend
how the lamentation transcendentally rises up over the regions
of human song, in order that we may make this elevation clear
by means of finest touch and tenderest intonation (the prescribed
ƒ must be regulated according to position and mood). The
first "Farewell" returns again, painfully changed by the surround-
ing harmony, but also the lament returns again. The rests require thoughtful lengthening; that becomes particularly evident
in the last measure.

The introduction has worked itself into the Allegro. In order

---

* Biography, Part II, Page 189.
† O. Jahn is opposed to this interpretation, and unjustly so, as is made manifest in the Biography, third edition, II, page 190.

to reproduce the passionate language of this scene, which reaches out amid an uprising and yielding, the utmost freedom is required, and the finest feeling for every part and for the melting together of all. The principal theme tarries with sharp intonation on the first tone, progresses from every first eighth (measure 1 and 2) to the second, perceptibly intones the first and third quarters, also every first eighth, tarries with emphasis on the first chord of measure 3, hesitates in the first three quarters, presses forward in the following two measures, the first with accompaniment of eighths, hesitates on the following *B*-octaves marked *sf*, and in the following measure, the fourth, with accompaniment of eighths.

Let this suffice. Complete analysis of tempo is impracticable, and would fetter one who attempted to follow closely, for indeed to give out free soul emotion, the soul of the interpreter must be free. Besides, the single moments of movement do not determine the picture (for they might be disputed here and there) so much as the absolutely free movement itself, which rises and falls with the surging of excitement, and never allows the charm of well-bred moderation to be forgotten. From measures 9 to 13 the duet inclination (with apology for the trivial trade name) begins to be felt. The close of the entire part hesitates. There is a peculiar significance in this movement of eighths, in the manner in which the voices separate and again cling together (measure 12), just as the maiden hangs upon the neck of her beloved and cannot let him go.

Now to the side theme, which expresses the unavoidable separation. The first "Farewell!" of the introduction is the heart of the side theme. It works itself up and down from the weeping middle voice, and perhaps one can guess at last a "We will meet again." The closing theme again depicts the pair, unable to part, each one clinging to the other.

These are the thoughts which form the first part of the movement. In the second part the principal theme appears again, intermingled with the "Farewell" from the introduction, whereupon the passage vanishes away. After the third part has again brought to recollection the first, the coda is formed from the "Farewell! We will meet again!" which with increasing certainty constitutes itself as the heart of the whole. Now it resounds from above, now from below; the feminine as well as the masculine voice is no longer a single melodic thread; it has become filled with harmony. And yet this simultaneous utterance of

two double voices is nothing more than the musically ideal picture of the two parting ones. Opposed to this, now below, now
above, there moves a counter theme in melting, progressive
eighths, passing with hurried flight, but ever with the characteristic grace of dignity.

That Beethoven has permitted the violent, ever eccentric im-
pulses of pain; that he has not, however, allowed this parting to
be intensified into convulsions of suffering; that he has clothed
these qualities, on the contrary, with the moderation and grace
of charming personalities, is a worthy feature of his artistic temperament. Impulsive characters revel insatiably in the pursual
of sorrow through all its distortions, while we attribute to colder
and weaker natures noble or even antique moderation, when in
truth—either from weakness or lack of moral courage—they
fail to perceive the truth, or lack means of expressing it. In the
past full truth was aimed at, regardless of moderation. Here
again the interpreter must follow the poet. The thought of parting (Coda)

must stand out gently, but above all in even movement, and in
slightly moderated tempo; the melody (consisting of the two
united upper voices) must, as the ➤ marks indicate, be uttered with a diminuendo; the eighths must flow on smoothly and
with utmost tenderness, with a soft emphasis on *a* and *a-flat*.
Feel the contents! Then, amid all the inadequacy of scattered
suggestions, the expression will come of itself.

Now the parting word resounds undisguisedly from both sides.
"Farewell!" calls the feminine voice. "Farewell!" answers the
masculine one, which we must imagine coming more and more
from a distance, therefore weaker. First the two voices sound
naturally simple, then ideal in their harmonic completeness; at
last, true to nature, they float into each other like calls of parting
ones—"Farewell!" and "Farewell, then!"

Here the poetic thought raises itself above harmonic law; two opposed harmonies, *b-flat—f* and *e-flat—g*, are sounded together. There was truth in the statement of Fetis, the eminent Conservatory director in Brussels, when he said, "If that is what is called music, it is not what *I* call music." It is not the music of Fetis, or of the French, or of the majority of musicians; it is the poesy, or, to speak more accurately, the transcendency of music which naturally lives in only a very few and can therefore be comprehended by only a few. If the interpreter has grasped Beethoven's thought, he can lead his hearers wherever he will. And finally we can say with Goethe:

> Who cannot understand me
> Must better learn to read.

The second movement is superscribed l'Absence. The deserted one feels the desolation of her loneliness. Here, of course, the duet form of the first movement must cease; only one principal voice manifests itself, but supported by a most sympathetic accompaniment. The first few measures

reveal the character of the entire movement. Beethoven names it "Andante expressivo," and adds "in progressive movement, but not without expression"—not that he tries uselessly to translate the well-known Italian expression, but to designate its innate activity. This idea of motion becomes especially manifest in the next to the lowest voice; in the painful interval (*e-flat—f-sharp*), this laborious progression, the feeling of desolation and loneliness is revealed as clearly as in the upper voice, which rises up and immediately after drops heavily and reaches most intense

expression in the close of the melody. The first chord in measure 1 and 2 must sound sharply, the first and third eighth, measure 3, must receive emphasis. But sufficient if not too much
guidance has been given, where the thought of the whole stands
out before the soul so clearly.

The third movement is a triumphal rejoicing of reunion, again
fashioned as a dialogue between the two lovers. Beethoven has
superscribed it with "Vivacissamente, in most rapid tempo."
This applies especially to the introduction; however, it might be
applied to the actual principal theme, the one in eighths, also to
the side theme in quarters; again, at the beginning of the second
part. For the passage of eighths ("I have thee again") even a
"poco Andante" is prescribed, and at the syncopated repetition
a further delay is essential. It would be incomprehensible if,
besides the delight, the tender emotion of the happy ones were
not also depicted.

E Minor Sonata Op. 90.*

Noble thought, energetic character speak out of the first
movement of this Sonata—it has only two movements. All that
impressive loquacity, in combat with painful doubt and hesitation, is able to do, comes to light in this movement. Feeling for
the individual moments, absolute freedom of treatment, and
added to this a fine comprehension for uniting all into unity—
these are requisites for the performer. Only a noble soul will be
able to follow Beethoven here.

The superscription "With animation and throughout with
feeling and expression," which the master intended for the entire
first movement, is especially applicable to the principal theme.
A most impressive persuasiveness determines and permeates the
many-membered theme, the construction and rhythm of which,
at least as regards the thesis, has been considered, pages 56 and
59. The antithesis (in two sections)

* Biography, Part II, Page 230.

is related to the thesis only by the rhythm of its first measure, then turns away from it in quiet, magnanimous resignation, in a progression which extends through nearly two octaves. The thought of the passage is lost if the player does not understand arriving at the *f-sharp* immediately after the $\overset{\lrcorner\,=}{c}$ *d-sharp* $\overset{=}{c}$ with absolute evenness and ease; more than that, to sound this *f-sharp* exactly together with the *c* and *c*, and still to lift it out above the accompanying mass. This quietness, following the impressive utterance of the thesis, is the stamp of a high-minded character which has power of aspiration, and yet, if need be, of resignation.

This resignation, however, is not absolute, for a second theme rises softly out of the deep, strengthens itself, and beats violently, very violently at its point of arrival. It was in vain, evidently, for the melody rolls down from its height into the depths, fades away after having consumed its entire power in progression, and the closing chords fall down powerlessly. The same thought, less high and less strong, repeats itself the third time lower, with less active rhythm, and this time marked p, in contrast to the first marked f and not sf. The last time it does not roll, but creeps down in continuous hesitation. This transition from desire to resignation, from forward pressing to receding, is the characteristic of the entire passage. The gradation of the thrice-uttered passage to the deeper register, regardless of the annotation, would solve itself on account of its position and manner of progression,—first full chords, then two tones; first a free utterance, then legato with the resting bass. Furthermore the manner of writing, viz.: sixteenths the first two times, then a sextolet and a quintolet; the last time sixteenths, a triplet of eighths, a quarter,—this is probably on account of more easy comprehension. In the first two runs, the tones should follow each other in an absolutely even passage which hastens its movement without any variety, and only delays the last tones on account of distinctness. There is no reason for making the sixteenths any different from the rhythm of six and five. The same is true in the third run, where the triplet of eighths and the quarter note appear. The run is to be taken from the beginning with a gradual, indeterminate retard, finally coming to a stop.

Even here, however, out of the *piano*, and out of the deep register, the thought rises once more, leads out in increasing power, step for step—now in B major—hesitating and halting, yet pressing forward up to the greatest embitterment—evidently in vain. A new theme (side theme, or second side theme, if the preceding may be considered as first) leads back to the deep register, with noble dignity but with irrevocable decision. The closing theme seems to state, sorrowfully but nobly, that the struggle was without victory, though not in vain. Strife to attain greatness and nobility is the work and content of life. Even Cato discovered that victory is not always granted by the God-head, in the manner in which we men had hoped and had considered just. That the closing theme speaks hesitatingly is very comprehensible.

This thoughtful hesitation leads into the second part. The principal theme—or at least the motive of its first sections—raises itself up again, not in its original freedom, but tied to continual eighth strokes. Nevertheless it struggles onward and attains great energy, but is soon compelled to return.

The remainder requires no further explanation; there are the same thoughts, though in other forms and other developments. Whoever has comprehended them once can follow them with certainty.

The energy which formed the principal content of the first movement has become exhausted with it. The second movement of the Sonata has therefore nothing of it. Here there is nothing but tenderness, gentle devotion, yea, sweetness of perception, the only content of which is resignation and rest, in gentle submission. Life often presents this phase, and that Beethoven has depicted here. More explicit directions for conception and interpretation would be superfluous.

A Major Sonata Op. 101.*

How difficult it is to steal quietly upon the most secret weavings of a tender soul possessed only of desire not of fulfillment, of aspiring fantasy, not of tangible ends or definite action— how difficult to draw to the light of day that which is not intended for daylight!

The very first movement "Allegretto ma non troppo," with additional superscription of "rather lively and with tenderest emotion" has, it is true, the ordinary form of a first sonata movement, not, however, its character, for it is rather an Adagio, a thought turned inward. It is a melody full of desire and longing; and the principal theme is based upon the dominant chord and its signification. But the melody does not move in one voice

---
* Biography, Part II. Page 232.

alone, for each of the voices has its significant and similarly
minded song beside the principal voice; and the movement
throughout is full of soul, full of sympathetic relationship and
melody. Added to this, there exists throughout a nervous excit-
ability, even breathlessness, which overcomes every closing point;
so a thoughtful delay (measure 4 on the last three eighths, measure 5 especially on the last three eighths, measure 6 throughout,
measure 9 on the first tone, measure 12, 15, and 16 likewise, then
measure 19 on the first tone, which closes the theme) may often
be suitable in this restless wave play. This excitement is more
of an internal character, it would rather conceal itself than become visible; a life apparently with no outward aim, but turned
and locked up within itself. It is, therefore, life inexhaustible;
the close (measure 19) becomes a deceptive close, the melody of
the voices flows on, once more seeks a close (measures 24 and 26),
and finds it at last in measure 28 All this space is required for
this one quiet, secret emotion, without change, almost without
intensification! It is the uncommunicative, taciturn spirit of an
Ottilie, but without the storms which this most admirable crea-
tion of Goethe was obliged to experience.

The side theme, which Beethoven has especially marked
"Expressivo e semplice," continues to relate the same narrative.
Indeed, in this tender soul there is no particular event, for the
soul itself is the only content, only that the emotion is even gen-
tler and seems to rest entirely in the syncopations.

In the second part the principal theme soars upward over
the roaring deep. Here follows the first moment in which this
vanishing quality rises to metallic power; the second moment
grows out of the far-reaching syncopations (page 5 of the original
edition of Steiner). All the rest belongs to the quiet of the beginning. A deep and essential characteristic of the whole is the
fact that this quiet development rises from the tenderest beginning to a most impressive intensity. The thought here expressed
should stand out tenderly, even nervously, but not powerlessly.
A lack of power may call forth regret, not, however, that sympathy which Beethoven wishes to call forth. It remains for the
player to bring out the tenderest passages through finely-tem-
pered, yet perceptible emphasis, while for the more intense portions he must cause the power to be anticipated by means of an
accelerated movement. It is essential, too, that in this intensification of power the original tenderness be not forgotten. In
none of the compositions considered thus far has it been so im-

portant to keep an even tempo and yet to make use of the tenderest wave line of rising and sinking; in fact, to keep from all
decided changes and striking contrasts.

The signs of innate power have not been deceptive; for the
second movement, which with Beethoven is usually a Scherzo, if
not an Adagio, enters here as a march ("Lively; Like a March").
But what a march! There is nothing of splendor or resistance,
or of the materiality of the combined power of a multitude, which
is the content of every march, even the Funeral March of the
Sonata Op. 26. Not outward deeds are here pictured, but rather
a fantasy of deeds which might happen, imaginary triumphal
processions, but such as would reach boldly to the stars.

A strange picture indeed is this triumphal procession, which
can take place only in imagination. It is all boldness: the sudden beginning, the sudden continuation from one broad accent
to another, the continuous pressing forward of the melody, and
the rising of the bass through three octaves. All this, however,
is executed more spiritually than physically. The first chords
are marked *f* and *sf,* but these are immediately followed by
p; then comes a *cres.,* but it does not lead to *forte,* but into a
tone region which is incapable of special strength. Soon after
the first *cres.* there follows a second which, however, leads to a
specially prescribed *piano.* All this is not the result of the
superscription merely, but is contained in, and necessarily
founded upon, the contents. It is as though bold resolutions and
violent words were mysteriously whispered into one's ear. The
player, who with this Sonata, as with all the last of Beethoven's,
must be beyond all preparatory training, may dream himself into
this bold mystery.

This is the nature of the entire March. The character of the
picture is completed by the interweaving of two or three independent voices in place of the one principal voice which might
be followed without any difficulty. And when at last the second
part rises up to a tangible height and remains there (the fifth
from the last measure), the bold step sinks back from tone-height
and modulation into the subdominant, into the dusk of resignation.

Strangely foreign is the Trio (again asking pardon for so mechanical a name) as it enters, and with its two canonlike and
long-drawn-out voices, darkly and searchingly seeks a close to
these unaccustomed and bold stories. And yet they return.

Is it repentance which speaks out of the third movement? Is

it a feeling of pain, a feeling that time and power for actual deeds
has vanished? Who would venture to uncover all the mysteries
of this tone life? Beethoven has superscribed the movement
"Slowly and longingly." Whatever the meaning may be, the
plaintive tone of the theme must be perceived and felt by everyone who approaches such works.

It is the return to self which has been accomplished here, and
this fact is verified by the circumstance that the introduction of
the last movement recalls the first movement through its principal theme. Here a rich, refreshing stream of life pours forth
with fresh courage, and now and then glittering with bright lights.
Nevertheless it is a spiritual life, a disembodied spiritual life, as
it were, as we now and then picture it in fancy, rather than an
echo of real life through which we struggle materially, whether
it be happy or sorrowful.

B-flat Major Sonata Op. 106.*

If the preceding Sonata dwells in the tenderest regions of soul
life, and almost vanishes away into the disembodied, then indeed
the large B-flat Major Sonata develops toward all sides a mass
of power without equal, spiritually or materially. It has been
called the "Giant Sonata," but such names (we have met others
of a similar nature, pages 117 and 130) are rather doubtful. It
certainly is true, however, that a giant spirit here exercises gigan-
tic members. The player must be possessed of the greatest technical power. He must also be prepared to bring forth large and
numerous tone masses, well separated from each other, each well
held together within itself; they must be well marshaled, one
against another, like strong armies. In this Sonata all is laid out
powerfully and broadly; not only are the powerful passages possessed of intense vibration, but also the tender ones, as in the
Adagio, which breathes out longing and complaint like a sigh, as
it were, inexhaustibly, out of the most secret depths of the soul.
The player must be watchful, not only of the details, but also of
the construction of the whole and relationship of the different
members to it.

The first movement is an Allegro. With a bold sweep from
out of the depths, and with a violent stroke, the first principal
theme enters and completes itself unexpectedly with soft tenderness, full of desire. The beginning (four measures) was power-

---

* Biography, Part II. Page 265.

ful with vibrations, the continuation suddenly soft and moderated;
but the melody presses firmly upward, and the bass marches
freely and in independent significance down from height to
depth. This last theme—the first entrance seems to be forgotten—is repeated in higher tone regions and with more ardent
and unceasing desire, up to the full close in B-flat major.

Here, however, in the closing tone itself, a second principal
theme appears, which repeats its main content (two measures)
four times, each time intensified, then grandly works itself upward with the last motive (but by no means hurriedly). Now it
descends and hovers thoughtfully over height and depth, now
becoming quiet, now hesitating, but constantly in a grand figure,
finally making a long sweep in double octaves. This second
principal theme may serve to represent, in broad dimensions, the
power of the introductory four measures of the Allegro; but it is
by no means similar to the first thought, which is full of vibrating, rhythmic energy.

Let us consider the dimensions of the movement. The first
principal theme consists of four measures (the entrance) plus 13
measures (the continuation), that is, 17 measures in all. The
second principal theme up to its close has 18 measures, and still
the principal subject is not finished. We will not continue counting measures, but it is well for the player to become acquainted
with the outward form of the work. Thus far the player has required power of attack for the first four measures, a leading onward and further intensification of the melody and bass, raising
them from quiet to intensity. Each of the four sections with
which the second principal theme opens must enter powerfully,
and from here on with broad resonance must return to *piano.*
Each of the sections must be a united whole and every entrance
must not only result in intensified power, but the whole subject
must appear as a whole, by means of evenness of performance
and equality of intensification, as, finally, through an even going-
to-rest at the close.

Now, at last, the spontaneous entrance of the first theme appears again, cyclically binding together the principal subject
however, in accordance with its violent character, it throws the
modulation with one progression from B-flat, which up to this
time has been the firmly held key, into D major. Evidently D
major is not the intended resting place, for out of *d—f-sharp—a*
there grows *d—f-sharp—a—c,* and we are settled in G major.
Twenty-four measures are used for this, or rather, three different

passages are fastened to each other. The first has the up-beat of
the bass taken from the introduction to the motive; the second
an anapestic motive ( ) which afterward comes to light in
the side theme; the third has running passages of eighths with
an opposing bass. This far-reaching leading into a side theme is
not generally Beethoven's characteristic; the side theme usually
enters without preparation, or else the principal theme flows
fluently from its own motives into the others. In the B-flat Sonata, however, proportion and character are differently determined, all verges into the extreme, the Titanic.

Now the side theme enters, first in the tenor or high bass,

recklessly throwing the close into the three-lined octave. There
appears also the far-reaching, running repetition. It streams
from the heights to the depths, hesitates a moment on *c* (C
major), again seizes the first motive and works with increasing
power and with firm strokes upward once more. Again it is essential that the player gather together the manifold and far-
reaching parts into a unit. Many a performer who can swim
over playful streams is not able to encounter these ocean waves.
A quiet first closing theme gives rest to thought and feeling; but
immediately there follows a second closing theme, beautiful in
its strength and in the happy feeling of its power. It leads back
to the beginning, to the repetition of the first part. Then it leads
into the second part; both times the motive avails itself of the
opportunity of soaring upward.

Here, first of all, a technical remark must be permitted.
Beethoven places the motive twice, first in one voice, then two-
voiced, and indeed, so

that finally the high notes (*g—g*) come in the left hand; and
this manner of playing should not be changed for any conven-
ience. The thought of the motive demands a stroke, a violent
emphasis upon the first of the high tones, upon *b-flat*, then upon
d̄, and finally upon *ḡ*. The left hand uses for these tones the
thumb, the most powerful finger for producing a stroke; the right
hand, however, would take it with the little finger, therefore with
the weakest finger.

After these calls, a broad mass of tone is again unfolded.
The motive (the first measure) of the introduction enters softly
this time, marked *p* and *sempre p*, and is developed for ten
measures (including the coda and free ending) by two voices in
canonform and in deep register. The passage is in E-flat major,
and closes in B-flat major; not until measure 7 is a cres. prescribed. From the closing point in B-flat the canonlike, free,
rather imitative passage repeats itself in two upper voices,
strengthened by a free voice and marked here *cres. piu.* Finally
it is repeated, and this time marked *f* with a doubling of the
two canonlike voices in a broad register, and again in similar
manner, with closer, and therefore sharper, duplication. This
doubling at first has the breadth of only a tenth, increased another octave, then the breadth of a third. This last doubling of
voices, after a short *piano* which is again followed by *cres.*,
is again marked *f*, with intensification (*sf*) of single moments,
therefore with a more significant *forte* than the first. Now at
last there follows, after the call which has introduced the part,
a *fortissimo*, as the climax of the whole development of 40
measures.

It is clear that in order to do justice to such great masses,
step for step, in their unity and progression, the most careful
weighing of the means must be exercised on the part of the performer. The right comprehension of single moments, even of all
single moments, will not by any means suffice; for the whole
must be represented and be made comprehensible in its unity

and life. First, the canonlike (or imitative) theme, up to its free
close (measure 7) must be conceived as a single melody

and interpreted through soulful intonations, through phrasing,
and through the tapering off of every moment (*a b-flat*). Then,
too, the imitative voice must follow, not merely the tone progressions, but also the manner of playing the first, even though by so
doing the intensities of one voice

do not fall together with those of the other, for example, in the
carrying out of the decres. (=-). Thus, throughout the entire
movement, every single voice must be perceived and compared
with the others. Then the gradations of the whole, the two,
three, and four-voiced passages, aside from the intonation of the
parts, must receive three rising gradations of intensity. Here
not only Beethoven's annotations, but his treatment of the subject, comes to the rescue. He places his thoughts—not only in
this Sonata, but in every deeply conceived work—first in transparent simplicity, then he adds more and more; and all can readily be comprehended because each succeeding step was prepared.

But will the power of the instrument permit of so great an intensification?

It will not! Therefore we must find other means. It has
been stated (page 76) that intensity of movement will assist intensity of power; indeed, thanks to the spiritual relationship of
things, it is more readily and deeply effective than the mass
power of sound, and must not be used except with the utmost
caution. I would consider it right to hold back at the above-

cited (page 149) introductions to the first motive, and to lengthen the rests, especially the last. Then the two-voiced passage would receive somewhat less movement than the original tempo indicated. From here on the motion would almost impercepti- bly, and with many a moment of delay, become more pressing, and in the doubling of the voices in thirds, would become more fiery.

I close here. Whoever has comprehended these fundamental principles will find no especial difficulty in their application to other works; on the other hand, one who could not make them his own would not be benefited by again as many individual re- marks.

One thing, I think, should be fully recognized and taken to earnest reflection in the study of this Sonata; for in this compre- hensive task it should become clear that feeling alone does not suffice for the greater demands of interpretation. Without the union of feeling with creative fancy there is no artist, no work of art, and no true interpretation; however, in the higher and richer tasks, there must be added, for the poet as well as for the inter- preter, deep insight and mature powers of comprehension, if the structure is to be a complete one according to laws of reason, and if it is to come to full representation and recognition in its reasonableness.

Close.

After the B-flat Major Sonata there still remain four of the
most important piano works: The E-major Sonata Op. 109, the
A-flat Major Sonata Op. 110, the C-minor Sonata Op. 111, the
Thirty-three Variations on a Waltz, Op. 120, and they are truly
invaluable gifts for any musician and lover of art who is able to
undertake them. How much might be said about them—how
much more than the little for which the Biography could give
room! Truly a desire for saying more was not wanting.

However, the aim held in view for this little book must have
attained its end in the study of this most powerful work (B-flat
Sonata), preceded as it was by works in which so much tenderness and many other qualities predominated. The object has
been reached in so far as it was in my power at all to arrive at
the heart of these works. To lead into the soul of Beethoven
and into the world created by him—that was my ambition; and
the only means for accomplishing this seemed to be to awaken a
consciousness for the contents, to open the eyes to self-contem-
plation, and to guide the spirit to self-recognition. He alone
who has experienced this can work independently and can progress from what he has recognized to further problems. If this
object has been attained, all further guidance could bring about
only an indolent and fettered dependence. Let every path lead
us away from this into freedom!

www.ingramcontent.com/pod-product-compliance
Lightning Source LLC
Chambersburg PA
CBHW030557270326
41927CB00007B/959

9783744796026